H. Owen Reed
Robert G. Sidnell

Michigan State University

The Materials of Music Composition

Book I: Fundamentals

Addison-Wesley Publishing Company

Reading, Massachusetts

Menlo Park, California • London • Amsterdam • Don Mills, Ontario • Sydney

Preface

This is the first book in a series of books about music. We have written this series for all people interested in how music is put together. It is, therefore, intended for a broad range of instructional settings. While no book or series of books can be all things to all students, we have attempted to select, sequence, and present clearly the important information regarding musical structure. Our goal is to sample from all of music to arouse honest intellectual curiosity about music practice. The proper study of music *is* music. We view music in its totality: Jazz, rock, pop, folk, art, and various non-Western types form our bases of study.

This series of books is organized in a cyclic fashion. The five basic parameters of music manipulated by composers, arrangers, and performers are presented in an ever-increasing degree of sophistication as the series unfolds. The parameters are: *rhythm*, *harmony*, *melody*, *form*, and *color*. As each parameter is revisited in each book, the material is accordingly more advanced and complex. Successful completion of all levels would insure a high degree of knowledge about music and its materials and an ability to use this knowledge in solving all kinds of musical problems. Each book is discrete unto itself but prerequisite to those that follow. A comprehensive *Instructor's Resource Guide*, designed for each book in the series, is available through the publisher.

Book I is a fundamentals book: It presumes little, if any, knowledge of music. Our point of departure is the nature and description of tone. The material in Book I forms the foundation for further study and includes creating, listening, and performing experiences. Because this is a fundamentals book, we assume no communication skill about music. This assumption limits the inclusion of many printed musical examples in this volume. We have included a broad sampling of jazz, pop, folk, and art music in the analytical listening sections of each chapter. Where possible and assuming minimum music reading skills, we have included printed music for illustrative purposes. Books II and III of the series include a wealth of all types of music both in score and suggestions for listening.

Book I has been successfully tested in classes ranging from high school performance classes to university theory classes. Like all the books in the series, it stresses the aural nature of music. That is, students develop their knowledge of music structure by learning to recognize and manipulate mentally certain aural phenomena: rhythms, chords, melodies, forms, and colors.

We believe that traditional theory courses are both unbalanced in subject matter and often unrealistic in addressing student needs. In the first instance, the usual heavy emphasis on harmony at the expense of equal treatment of the other parameters (melody, rhythm, form, color) results in an imbalance in functional musicianship. A close inspection of those parameters that tend to be omitted or slighted reveals much knowledge that is crucial to music learning. With regard to student needs, the vast majority of music learners are players and singers of a single musical line or melody, a fact ignored in many texts. Since we believe significant attention should be paid to *all* music students we have included much material that is geared to the needs of this majority.

This book, then, presents a balanced treatment of fundamental knowledge concerning the five parameters of music. At strategic points in each chapter, we have inserted self-testing sections called Check Your Understanding (CYU). These are designed to give students the opportunity to demonstrate competency to the instructor and to themselves before too much material has been covered. Answers for CYU's are included in Appendix 4.

Each chapter closes with a set of Activities for Developing Music Literacy (ADML). These drills fall into four parts, all devised to develop the aural, analytical, and creative capacities of music students:

1. Aural Drills (to include keyboard experience)
2. Analytical Listening
3. Improvisation
4. Creative Writing

We urge the instructor to use these activities at appropriate intervals to parallel and enrich the presentation of the written material. Thorough mastery of these materials is fundamental to the development of sensitive, understanding musicianship.

In addition to the definitions and descriptions supplied in the text, succinct definitions of important terms are readily available to the student in Appendix 1, which functions as both a glossary and an index. Terms printed in boldface type in the text are those contained in the Glossary/Index. These terms form the basis of fluent communication about music and its structure.

It is our sincere hope that all students and teachers of music will find the following presentation interesting, thorough, straightforward, and motivating.

ACKNOWLEDGMENTS

The authors' list of acknowledgments of assistance would be a long one if all who aided in this effort were noted. We would be remiss, however, if we did not express our gratitude to Dr. James Niblock, Chairman of Music, and to the faculty members in the departments of composition, music education, and music theory at Michigan

State University, for numberless comments and criticisms. We also owe special thanks to the following colleagues who advised us or tested this book in classes: Robert Agnew, Myron Colber, Robert Erbes, Burgess Gardner, Robert Hogenson, Kermit Holly, Russell Friedewald, Jere Hutcheson, David Lehr, James Leonard, Larry McClellan, Charles Ruggiero, Robert Sabourin, Merrell Sherburn, Greg A. Steinke, William Toutant, Lee Welch, David Wessel, and Michael A. Zinn.

East Lansing, Michigan   H. O. R.
September 1977   R. G. S.

Contents

INTRODUCTION

Characteristics of Musical Sound... 2
    Pitch/Intensity/Timbre/Duration
CYU No. 1.. 7
The Five Basic Parameters... 9
    Rhythm/Harmony/Melody/Form/Color
CYU No. 2...11

CHAPTER 1   RHYTHM

Pulse...14
Tempo..15
CYU No. 1...17
The Notation of Duration..19
    Writing Notes/Extended Duration
CYU No. 2...25
Meter..29
CYU No. 3...33
Motion...35
CYU No. 4...39
ADML: Aural and Keyboard Drill......................................41
ADML: Analytical Listening..47
ADML: Improvisation..48
ADML: Creative Writing..50

CHAPTER 2 HARMONY

The Notation of Pitch..52
CYU No. 1..55
Alteration Signs..57
CYU No. 2..59
Naming the Octaves..61
CYU No. 3..63
Clefs and Staffs..65
CYU No. 4..71
Intervals...75
   General Interval Size/Specific Interval Size
CYU No. 5..79
Inversion of Intervals..81
CYU No. 6..83
Triads..85
CYU No. 7..91
ADML: Aural and Keyboard Drill...................................95
ADML: Analytical Listening.......................................99
ADML: Improvisation...101
ADML: Creative Writing..102

CHAPTER 3 MELODY

Diatonic Scales and Modes.......................................104
CYU No. 1...109
Tetrachords and Diatonic Scale Construction.....................113
CYU No. 2...117
Major and Harmonic Minor Scales.................................121
CYU No. 3...125
Transposition of Scales and the Circle of Fifths................127
CYU No. 4...131
Key Signatures..135
Modal Key Signatures..137
CYU No. 5...139
ADML: Aural and Keyboard Drill..................................143
ADML: Analytical Listening......................................150
ADML: Improvisation...151
ADML: Creative Writing..152

CHAPTER 4 FORM

Form for the Creator 154
Variants of a Configuration and its Segments
CYU No. 1 163
Form for the Performer 167
CYU No. 2 169
Form for the Listener 171
CYU No. 3 173
ADML: Aural and Keyboard Drill 175
ADML: Analytical Listening 178
ADML: Improvisation 179
ADML: Creative Writing 180

CHAPTER 5 COLOR

Variation of Pitch 182
CYU No. 1 185
Variation of Intensity 187
CYU No. 2 191
Variation of Duration 193
CYU No. 3 197
Variation of Tempo 199
Variation of Timbre 200
CYU No. 4 203
ADML: Aural and Keyboard Drill 205
ADML: Analytical Listening 208
ADML: Improvisation 209
ADML: Creative Writing 209

APPENDIXES

Appendix 1: Glossary/Index 211
Appendix 2: Triad Nomenclature 223
Appendix 3: Source Material for Developing Music Literacy 224
Appendix 4: Answers to CYU's 225

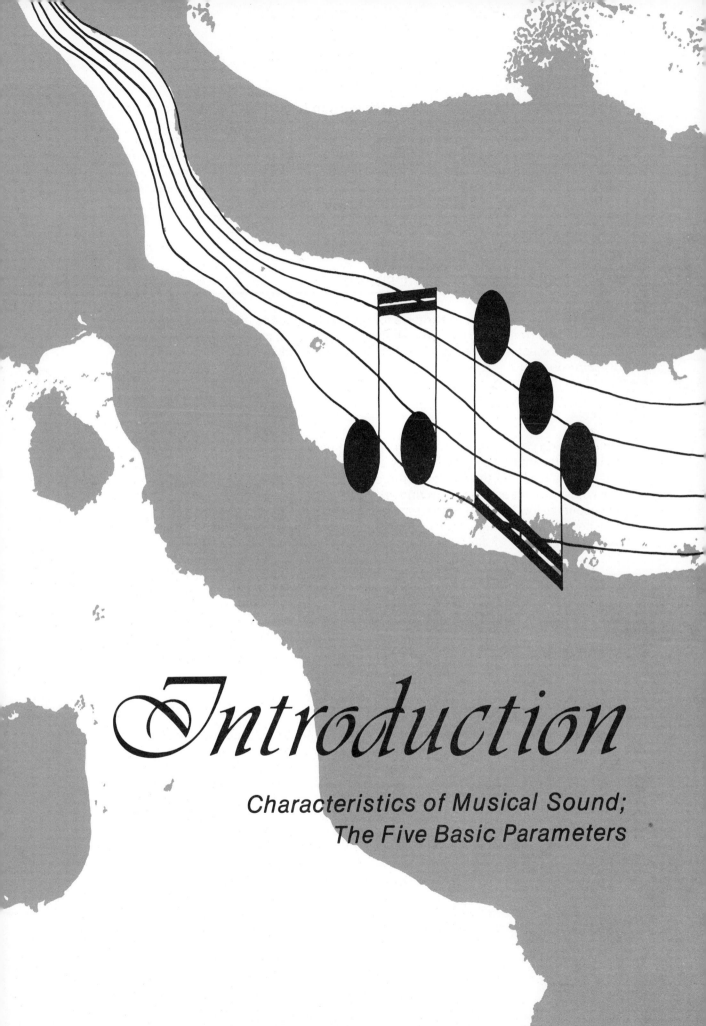

Introduction

Characteristics of Musical Sound;
The Five Basic Parameters

Music is made up of sound and silence occurring through time. The music creator—composer, improviser, or performer—arranges the sounds to occur in a preconceived sequence or, in the case of the improviser, a spontaneous flow. The sounds themselves are produced by a variety of vibrating devices: vocal cords, strings, columns of air, membranes, reeds, bars, plates, and electronic oscillators. Most musical sounds, known as **tones**, result from periodic vibrations. They are therefore distinctly different from other sounds, termed **noise**, which are nonperiodic. This does not mean that noise has no place in music, however, for many noise sources are used in musical composition.

CHARACTERISTICS OF MUSICAL SOUND

Scientists* who study sound attribute four characteristics to musical tone: **pitch, intensity, timbre** (tone color), and **duration.**† The first three characteristics are useful in describing the nature of a tone while the fourth, duration, refers to the length of time a tone is sounded.

Pitch

Pitch is a term used to describe the relative highness or lowness of a tone. The level of pitch is determined by the **frequency** of vibrations, and the differences we hear between two pitches are the result of different frequencies of vibration. People refer to a tone with many vibrations per second as high in pitch, and to one with few vibrations per second as low in pitch. Some people can hear tones from a low pitch of 16 vibrations per second to a high pitch of 20,000 vibrations per second. Piano pitches range from approximately 27 vibrations per second to 4192 vibrations per second.

The basic unit of frequency, one vibration per second, is called a **hertz** (Hz), in honor of the 19th century physicist H. R. Hertz. The tuning note for most orchestras is A = 440 Hz, while middle C on the piano is most often tuned to about 262 Hz. The various human voices range from about 28 Hz for a low bass to about 1048 Hz for the soprano. The tuba spans an approximate range of 40 Hz to 262 Hz. The flute spans a range from middle C‡ (262 Hz) to three octaves above middle C (2096 Hz).

Intensity

Intensity is a term used to describe the relative loudness or softness of tones. The vibrating motion of a string, bar, or other object sets off in the air a train of disturbances known as a **sound wave.** The degree of intensity perceived by a listener depends on the **amplitude** of the sound wave as it is picked up by the ear. The bigger the amplitude of the sound wave, the stronger or more intense the sound. Thus, people describe sounds produced by waves of great amplitude as very loud sounds. A simple experiment with a violin string will demonstrate this point. If you pluck one of the strings lightly, you will see the string move only slightly from its position of rest. On the other hand, if you pluck the string vigorously, you will see great displacement of the string and you will perceive a louder sound.

---

*   We are indebted to Professors Dale Bartlett and Owen Jorgensen of Michigan State University for their advice on **acoustical** matters.

†   We are aware of the discrepancy between physical and perceptual terminology but have chosen our terms for ease of comprehension in this fundamental presentation.

‡   Refer to Example 2.7 for the identification of middle C.

The intensity of tone is measured in **decibels** (db). A decibel is approximately the smallest change in loudness that the ear can detect under normal conditions. Common environmental and musical sounds are included in Example I.1 to illustrate different levels of intensity.

Example I.1
The Intensity of Various Sounds*

TYPE OF SOUND	LEVEL IN DECIBELS	DISTANCE AWAY
Moon rocket at lift-off	200	300 meters
Jet aircraft taking off	140	25 meters
Very noisy factory	100	0 meters
Orchestra at loud level	100	near conductor
Ringing alarm clock	80	1 meter
Normal conversation	65	1 meter
Orchestra at soft level	60	near conductor
Still day away from traffic	25	0 meters

Composers and performers use variations in intensity freely to make music more expressive. Within the last century, composers have grown very specific in indicating levels of loudness of their music.

Timbre (Tone Color)

The third characteristic of musical tone is **timbre** or **tone color.** Timbre refers to the specific sound quality of a given instrument or voice. Each instrument and voice displays a different **spectrum**, or combination of **harmonics**, which partially accounts for the different qualities heard by listeners. Thus, in order to understand differences in tone quality, a basic understanding of the nature of harmonics is necessary.

A musical tone, while perceived as having a single pitch or frequency, is in reality produced by a composite of many frequencies. When a tone is sounded, the ear usually focuses primarily on one frequency and to a lesser degree on a host of others. The predominant frequency heard is called the **fundamental**, or the first harmonic. The less discernible frequencies are designated the second, third, fourth, etc. harmonics. The quality of the tone is partly caused by the pattern and relative strengths of these harmonics. In the case of a violin string, when the string is set in vibration, it vibrates in two ways: as a whole string and in many parts. Vibrations of the whole string account for the pitch perceived, while vibrations of the parts are responsible for other harmonics that color the sound and help to make it distinctly a violin tone in quality. At least sixteen harmonics, known collectively as a **harmonic series**, assist in the coloration of a musical tone. Example I.2 illustrates this concept.

---

* These data are taken from Rupert Taylor, *Noise* (New York: Penguin Books, 1970) and John Backus, *The Acoustical Foundations of Music* (New York: W. W. Norton, 1969).

Example I.2
The Harmonic Series on C2

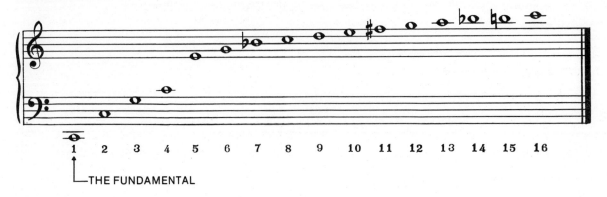

Example I.3
Sound Spectra for Various Instruments Playing E♭4*

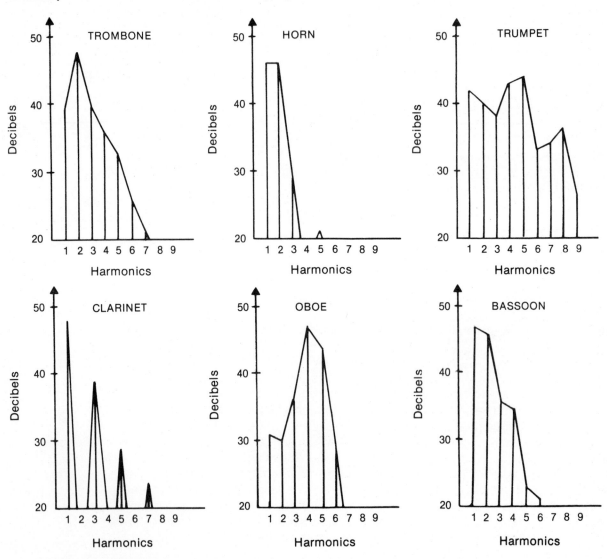

---
*   These data are the result of timbre research by Professor Davis Wessel, Department of Psychology, Michigan State University, 1974.

For present purposes, the relative intensities of the harmonics shown in Example I.2 are not an important issue. But note the diagrams in Example I.3, which show the sound spectra of different instruments playing the same pitch. The perceived differences in quality result from differences in the relative strengths of various harmonics in the spectrum for each instrument.

The human voice functions in the same way as other musical instruments. The sound spectra for a bass, a tenor, an alto, and a soprano, each singing an "ah" vowel on the pitch middle C, would be different from one another. Different vowels, different pitches, and different voice types would all display different sound spectra. In each voice, certain harmonics would be relatively weaker or stronger and would thus produce differences in quality.

Duration

The final characteristic of musical tone is duration, or the relative length of a tone. Composers indicate various durational values through notation. Actual durations are subject to the interpretation of the performer and are affected, sometimes adversely, by **tempo** and **accent**.

STAFF FOR SKETCHING

CHECK YOUR UNDERSTANDING

Introduction, No. 1

1. Name six vibrating devices that can produce sound.

   _____   _____

   _____   _____

   _____   _____

2. Tones result from _____ vibrations of sound-producing devices.

3. List the four characteristics of tone.

   _____   _____

   _____   _____

4. We refer to a tone with many vibrations per second as _____ in pitch.
   (high or low)

5. What is the name of the unit of frequency?

   _____   _____
   (full name)   (abbreviation)

6. What term is used to describe the relative loudness or softness of a tone?

   _____

7. Sound sensations result from _____ picked up by the ear.

8. The louder sounds are produced by sound waves of _____
   (greater or smaller)
   amplitude.

9. The intensity of sound is measured in units called

   _____   _____
   (full name)   (abbreviation)

10. The difference in the sound of a trumpet and a violin playing the same pitch is

    due primarily to a characteristic of music tone known as _____.

    It is also sometimes called _____ _____.

11. When a single tone is produced on a trombone, for instance, the ear focuses on a
    single frequency of a very complex sound spectrum. This predominating fre-

    quency is called the _____ and the entire complex

    of frequencies is called the _____ _____.

12.   Another characteristic of tone, that concerned with its relative length, is

_____.

13.   Among the following, underscore only those terms or symbols that refer to *intensity*.

timbre   duration   spectrum   hertz   harmonics   pitch
decibel   amplitude   frequency   loudness   tempo

THE FIVE BASIC PARAMETERS

The basic dimensions of music can be reduced to five parameters: **rhythm, harmony, melody, form,** and **color.** A **parameter** is an element that can be controlled. Musical style is a product of the choice of materials and the interaction of parameters within a composition. In this book we deal with each of the above five parameters as we show how materials are used by composers in the organization of sound. Other variables, such as **texture,** * will be discussed as they relate to the five basic parameters. A preliminary definition of each parameter is given below, and the chapters of this book provide a first encounter with each parameter at its most basic level.

Rhythm

Entire books have been written in an attempt to define rhythm adequately, but simply stated this parameter encompasses all time elements of music. Only the basic, structural elements that organize music into an aural-time art are discussed in this book. We are first of all concerned with a clear understanding of the way music is structured in terms of pulse, tempo, meter, and durations of sounds and silences. These characteristics are discussed in Chapter 1.

Harmony

Harmony is the study of the vertical structure of music in **chords (triads, seventh chords,** and other vertical stackings of tones) and of the horizontal movement of chords. In order to discuss chords and chord connection, we must first explain how pitch is notated on the staff. This we do in Chapter 2. In addition to pitch notation, we examine how simple harmonies are produced as **harmonic intervals** and triads.

Melody

Melody is an orderly, horizontal succession of tones heard as the dominating **line.** Preliminary to the writing of melodies is an understanding of **scale** construction, **key signatures,** and **melodic intervals.** Chapter 3 sets forth the various kinds of **tetrachords** and ways of combining them to form new as well as traditional scales used in the construction of melodies.

Form

The study of musical form is a study of the growth of initial musical gestures (**configurations**) into larger formal units. In Chapter 4 we look at some of the ways composers achieve this, and we survey the need for form in music. As we shall see, every detail of form becomes important in composing, interpreting, and listening.

---

*   The manner in which sounds are interwoven. We speak of a *thin* texture or a *thick* texture; of **monophonic** texture (single melodic line), **polyphonic** texture (two or more melodic lines combined), and **homophonic** texture (simultaneous sounding of other tones in support of a melodic line, that is, *chordal* texture).

Color

Color, in its broadest meaning, is defined in the *American Heritage Dictionary* as "variety of effect or expression," and "the use of realistic or picturesque detail." This book will deal with the color parameter in only its most elementary aspects: the variation of pitch (through **vibrato**, etc.), the variation of intensity (**dynamic** changes), the variation of duration (using different types of **articulation**), the variation of tempo (using terms that indicate tempo modification), and the variation of timbre (tone quality). These factors aid the performer, the improviser, and the composer in coloring tones and moulding otherwise dull music into something exciting and captivating.

As we have indicated, in Book I we examine the five basic parameters from only the most fundamental perspective. Throughout the book we provide frequent opportunities to check your understanding, and at the end of each chapter we provide activities that will help you gain a more thorough knowledge of the essential resources necessary to create, perform, and listen to music with understanding.

CHECK YOUR UNDERSTANDING
Introduction, No. 2

1. Name the five basic parameters in music. _____
    _____   _____
    _____   _____

2. Name the five ways of enhancing the expressive qualities of music.
    _____   _____
    _____   _____
    _____

3. The parameter concerned with the vertical stacking of tones to form chords and
    with the relationship of one chord to another is called _____

4. The parameter concerned with the orderly horizontal succession of tones is
    called _____

5. When we consider the way music grows from an initial idea, we refer to this pro-
    cess as the _____ parameter.

6. The fifth parameter, which deals with the expressive elements in music, is
    called _____

7. Among the following, underscore only those terms or symbols that refer to
    rhythm.

    pitch   tempo   timbre   meter   harmonic series   tone color
    intensity   sound wave   spectrum   decibel   hertz   pulse

STAFF FOR SKETCHING

Chapter 1

Rhythm

*Pulse; Tempo; The Notation of
Duration; Meter; Motion*

Music is an aural and temporal art. Sounds and silences are produced by performers in certain ways as specified by composers and/or by performers themselves. The latter occurs in jazz and many other improvisational, **indeterminant** (chance) musical events in both Western and non-Western music. Perhaps the most important of the organizational parameters of music is the way musical time is ordered. This is the parameter called **rhythm.**

Rhythm, as we use the term, encompasses all of the temporal aspects of music. Specifically, for present purposes we define rhythm as the combined effect of all factors contributing to the organized flow of sound and silence durations in time. This definition differs from the narrow point of view regarding rhythm, which deals simply with durational sound patterns.

PULSE

Pulse is, by definition, the basic temporal element in a music event. Generally, pulse divides a period of time into small units of equal and sometimes unequal lengths. Pulses of equal duration are referred to as **periodic**, those of unequal duration as **nonperiodic**. The term **beat** is synonymous with pulse, and we use the term **unit** (or **unit of beat**) to signify the kind of note designated to receive one pulse (one beat). Finally, we define a **unit-pattern** as a pulse-sound or a group of sounds equivalent to one pulse, and we speak of a **rhythm-pattern** as a group of sounds made up of two or more unit-patterns.

The identification of pulse within a musical event is, of course, an aural perception. As Murphy has stated, "listening is undeniably the sole basis of musical experience."* Listeners bring both cultural and personal experiences to the event and are free to "tap their feet as they wish." For example, try listening to the recording of Bach's *D Minor Invention*† as performed on a music synthesizer where dynamic **accent** is lacking. How do you feel the pulse? Do you hear two or six sounds per pulse in the beginning? In the absence of a score, either response could be correct.

The placement of pulse is fundamental to the listening and performing experience. When a listener hears a series of rapid, equally spaced sounds, it is natural to group them into pulses. Most often each pulse contains an equal number of such sounds. It is quite possible, however, to have unequal numbers in each pulse. (See Example 1.1) Listeners tend to group sounds into pulses on the basis of several perceptual clues. Often there will be some evidence of **stress**, or emphasis, at the start of a pulse. If not, the listener may imagine it exists. Also, the *speed* at which the sounds move through time provides important aural information to the listener. But even with these clues in evidence, it is possible for different listeners to group the number of sounds per pulse differently: periodically (2 + 2) or nonperiodically (2 + 3, 3 + 2). As a matter of fact, composers often try to mask or vary sound groupings for the express purpose of increasing interest in their music.

A short recorded excerpt of fast dripping water will elicit a variety of responses from separate listeners when they are asked to organize the dripping sounds into pulses. Consider Example 1.1.

---

*   Howard Murphy, *Teaching Musicianship* (New York: Coleman Ross, 1950), p. 60.

†   J. S. Bach, "Invention in D Minor," in *Switched on Bach*. Performed by Walter Carlos, Columbia MS7194, 1968.

Example 1.1
Deriving Pulse from Equally Spaced Sounds

M. M. ' = 240

	Sounds	'	'	'	'	'	'	'	'	'	'	'	'

PERIODIC

4 to a pulse	' ' '
3 to a pulse	' ' ' '
2 to a pulse	' ' ' ' ' '
6 to a pulse	' '

NONPERIODIC

3 + 2 to a pulse	' ' ' ' '
2 + 3 to a pulse	' ' ' ' '

TEMPO

One of the basic pulse variables is **tempo**—the **pace** of music. The most natural tempos reflect the basic body rhythms of heartbeat, breathing, and walking. All of these body activities occur at a slow to moderate rate. Today, music is performed at a broad range of tempos from 40 to 180 pulses per minute. Pulses at a pace faster than 180 per minute tend to be perceived as divisions of a slower basic pulse. Pulses at tempos below 40 per minute are too slow to be perceived as the basic pulse of a musical event.

This large range of tempos did not always exist. In the 15th and 16th centuries, for example, pulse was relatively fixed at about 60 per minute. Changes in tempo were accomplished by manipulating the rhythmic patterns to give the illusion of faster or slower tempos. As musical practice in the Western world became more sophisticated, the need for precise tempos became apparent. Today, composers are extremely sensitive regarding the right tempos for their music.

An important invention in the early 19th century facilitated exactness in tempo. The invention was the **metronome**, devised by **Maelzel** in 1816. At the beginning of music, it is common to see a notation such as M.M. ♩ = 60, although the abbreviation M.M. is often omitted today. The letters M.M. refer to Maelzel's Metronome, which sounds pulses at a preset rate of so many beats per minute. With or without the help of this device, it is important for students of music to develop a keen sense of tempo. A good beginning is to imagine a pulse of 60 beats per minute—one per second. From this basic pace, a tempo of 120 (twice as fast), or 180 (three times as fast) can be derived.

Tempo has an important influence on an individual's perception of pulse. For example, how would you perceive the pulse in each of the following?

Example 1.2
Sensing Pulse

a) ' = 60

'   '   '   '   '   '   '   '   '   '   '   '   Sounds

'   '   '   '   '   '   '   '   '   '   '   '   12 pulses perceived

b) ' = 120

| ' | ' | ' | ' | ' | ' | ' | ' | ' | ' | ' | ' | Sounds |

'	'	'	'	'	'	'	'	'	'	'	'	12 pulses perceived
												or
'			'			'			'			4 pulses perceived

c) ' = 180

| ' | ' | ' | ' | ' | ' | ' | ' | ' | ' | ' | ' | Sounds |

'			'			'			'			4 pulses perceived
												or
'				'				'				3 pulses perceived

Most listeners would hear Example 1.2 (a) as twelve separate pulses. They could hear Example 1.2 (b) in either of two ways. Some listeners might, again, hear 12 separate pulses, while others might argue for four pulses with a division of each pulse into a unit-pattern of three sounds. In Example 1.2 (c), at a faster tempo (180 per minute), the average listener will probably sense four pulses with divisions in threes, three pulses with divisions into fours, or possibly six pulses with divisions into twos.

As this example illustrates, the relationship of tempo to pulse is a matter of individual interpretation. For performers, this factor becomes crucial. It bears directly on the way the music will be presented. Composers should therefore indicate very clearly the tempo at which they intend their music to move. The importance of this notion will be reinforced later in this chapter, under the discussion of meter.

Example 1.2 illustrates another point—the fact that very often a listener's ear may perceive something quite different from the written score with respect to pulse and pattern. In Example 1.2 (b), although we have no written score from which to verify which perception is correct, we know that the score can match only one of the perceptions. Often visual information from the conductor will affect the aural perception of the listener. For each listener, the deciding factor will probably be the pace of the music. There is, however, no need to belabor the issue of the difference between hearing and seeing music.

CHECK YOUR UNDERSTANDING

Chapter 1, No. 1

1. Rhythm is defined as _____

   _____

   _____

2. Pulse is defined as _____

   _____

3. Often, recurring pulses are of the same duration; however, there are many occasions when pulse can be _____ in duration.

4. The pace at which pulse moves is called _____

5. An important obligation for all composers is to indicate the _____ at which the music is supposed to move.

6. Define a unit-pattern.

   _____

7. Define a rhythm-pattern.

   _____

8. How might different listeners perceive the following group of twelve equally spaced sounds at the various tempos indicated?

   a) ' = 48

   '   '   '   '   '   '   '   '   '   '   '   '

   as _____ pulses

   b) ' = 240

   '   '   '   '   '   '   '   '   '   '   '   '

   as _____ sound(s) to a pulse or as _____ sound(s) to a pulse

   c) ' = 120

   '   '   '   '   '   '   '   '   '   '   '   '

   as _____ pulses with _____ sounds per pulse

   as _____ pulses with _____ sounds per pulse

   as _____ pulses with _____ sounds per pulse

   as _____ pulses with _____ sounds per pulse

9. A metronome is a device which provides performers with _____

   _____

10.   Find the approximate tempo indication for the following. *

a) your heartbeat _____

b) your breathing rate _____

c) your normal walking rate _____

d) the ticking of your wristwatch _____

11.   Among the following, underscore only those terms or symbols that refer to *rhythm*.

pulse   spectrum   unit of beat   intensity   unit-pattern   color
pitch   rhythm-pattern   tempo   nonperiodic beat   pace
harmonic series   periodic beat   metronome   db   accent
Hz   stress

(Be sure you can define all of the above.)

_____

*   An easy way to record tempo is to count the number of pulses in five seconds and multiply by twelve; or a simple pendulum can be constructed with a piece of string and a weight. Vary the length of the pendulum (string) until the desired tempo is attained. Count the number of complete cycles occurring in one minute, or count the number of cycles in five seconds and multiply by twelve.

THE NOTATION OF DURATION

Duration of musical sound and silence is indicated through a system of symbols called **notes** and **rests**. Notes are of several types, each representing a relative duration of musical sound.

Example 1.3
The Parts of a Note

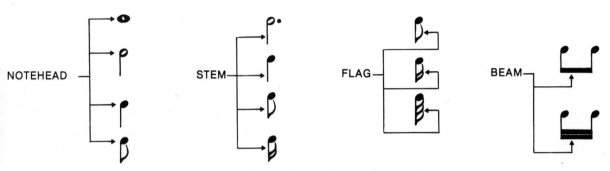

The most common system for naming notes is based on a fractional part of a whole, for example, eighth, quarter, half. A similar system is used to indicate durations of silence in music **notation**. Traditional notes and rests are shown in Example 1.4.

Example 1.4
Traditional Notes and Rests

SYMBOL FOR SOUND (NOTE)	SYMBOL NAME	SYMBOL FOR SILENCE (REST)
𝅝	Whole	▬
𝅗𝅥	Half	▬
𝅘𝅥	Quarter	𝄽
𝅘𝅥𝅮	Eighth	𝄾
𝅘𝅥𝅯	Sixteenth	𝄿
𝅘𝅥𝅰	Thirty-second	𝅀

Note and rest symbols in music represent a proportional system of sound or silence. This note symbol system is illustrated in Example 1.5.

Example 1.5
The Durational Relationship of Notes*

WHOLE	HALF	QUARTER	EIGHTH	SIXTEENTH	THIRTY-SECOND
1 =	2 =	4 =	8 =	16 =	32

Another note commonly used is the **grace note**. It has no measurable rhythmic value, but takes time from an adjacent note. Grace notes are written half-size. A single grace note is written as a small eighth note with a slash (♪). In groups of two or three, grace notes are written with two beams without a slash (♫   ♫♫). Groups of four or more require three beams (♫♫♫).

Example 1.6
The Durational Relationship of Rests

WHOLE	HALF	QUARTER	EIGHTH	SIXTEENTH	THIRTY-SECOND
1 =	2 =	4 =	8 =	16 =	32

---

*   Although rarely used, the chart would be correct with dots added to each of the notes.

In Example 1.5, the indication is that a single whole note has a durational value equal to two half notes, four quarter notes, eight eighth notes, sixteen sixteenth notes, or thirty-two thirty-second notes. Collectively, then, four quarter notes represent the same duration as a single whole note. This relationship can be expressed in an equation: $\frac{4}{4} = \frac{1}{1}$. Other similar equivalents can easily be deduced.

Example 1.6 illustrates the rest symbol system. As comparison with Example 1.5 will show, the relationship patterns for rests are the same as those for notes.

It is important to recognize that in the abstract, notes and rests indicate *relative* durations only. No specific duration can be assumed for any note or rest symbol unless more information is available. Thus it is grossly incorrect to assume that either the half note or the half rest is to receive a duration of "two." A half note has, quite simply, half the duration of a whole note. Similarly, a quarter note has half of whatever duration is designated for a half note. The exact duration is not known until an assignment of duration is made within the system. Once a duration is assigned to a specific kind of note the duration of any other note or rest can be determined. Careful study of Example 1.7 should make this notion clear.

Example 1.7
Relative Duration of Notes and Rests

If the note or rest below is assigned a value of 1 pulse...		then the symbol below has a duration of 2 pulses...		and the symbol below will have a duration of ½ pulse.	
NOTE	REST	NOTE	REST	NOTE	REST
♩	▬	𝅝	▬	♪	𝄿
♩	𝄽	♩	▬	♬	𝄾
♬	𝄾	♩	𝄽	♬	𝄿

The information contained in Examples 1.5 and 1.7 brings us to an understanding of durational note **division**. Note division is the fractional partitioning of duration. A quarter note can be divided into two eighth, four sixteenth, or eight thirty-second notes. Each level of **regular division** is achieved by dividing by two. **Dotted notes*** usually divide into threes as a first level division and into twos thereafter. (On occasion, dotted notes are divided by twos as first level division and undotted notes by threes.†) The

---

*　·　Dotted notes are explained on page 23.

†　　This kind of division, known as **irregular division** (or sometimes **borrowed division**), is discussed in Book II.

process of note division provides visual representation of unit-patterns in addition to the single pulse-sound. Information about regular note division is summarized in Example 1.8.

Example 1.8
First, Second, and Third Level Divisions of Selected Notes

NOTE	FIRST LEVEL DIVISION	SECOND LEVEL DIVISION	THIRD LEVEL DIVISION
𝅝	𝅗𝅥 𝅗𝅥	𝅘𝅥 𝅘𝅥 𝅘𝅥 𝅘𝅥	𝅘𝅥𝅮 𝅘𝅥𝅮 𝅘𝅥𝅮 𝅘𝅥𝅮 𝅘𝅥𝅮 𝅘𝅥𝅮 𝅘𝅥𝅮 𝅘𝅥𝅮
𝅗𝅥	𝅘𝅥 𝅘𝅥	𝅘𝅥𝅮 𝅘𝅥𝅮 𝅘𝅥𝅮 𝅘𝅥𝅮	𝅘𝅥𝅯 𝅘𝅥𝅯 𝅘𝅥𝅯 𝅘𝅥𝅯 𝅘𝅥𝅯 𝅘𝅥𝅯 𝅘𝅥𝅯 𝅘𝅥𝅯
𝅘𝅥	𝅘𝅥𝅮 𝅘𝅥𝅮	𝅘𝅥𝅯 𝅘𝅥𝅯 𝅘𝅥𝅯 𝅘𝅥𝅯	𝅘𝅥𝅰 𝅘𝅥𝅰 𝅘𝅥𝅰 𝅘𝅥𝅰 𝅘𝅥𝅰 𝅘𝅥𝅰 𝅘𝅥𝅰 𝅘𝅥𝅰
𝅝.	𝅗𝅥 𝅗𝅥 𝅗𝅥	𝅘𝅥 𝅘𝅥 𝅘𝅥 𝅘𝅥 𝅘𝅥 𝅘𝅥	𝅘𝅥𝅮 𝅘𝅥𝅮 𝅘𝅥𝅮 𝅘𝅥𝅮 𝅘𝅥𝅮 𝅘𝅥𝅮 𝅘𝅥𝅮 𝅘𝅥𝅮 𝅘𝅥𝅮 𝅘𝅥𝅮 𝅘𝅥𝅮 𝅘𝅥𝅮
𝅗𝅥.	𝅘𝅥 𝅘𝅥 𝅘𝅥	𝅘𝅥𝅮 𝅘𝅥𝅮 𝅘𝅥𝅮 𝅘𝅥𝅮 𝅘𝅥𝅮 𝅘𝅥𝅮	𝅘𝅥𝅯 𝅘𝅥𝅯 𝅘𝅥𝅯 𝅘𝅥𝅯 𝅘𝅥𝅯 𝅘𝅥𝅯 𝅘𝅥𝅯 𝅘𝅥𝅯 𝅘𝅥𝅯 𝅘𝅥𝅯 𝅘𝅥𝅯 𝅘𝅥𝅯
𝅘𝅥.	𝅘𝅥𝅮 𝅘𝅥𝅮 𝅘𝅥𝅮	𝅘𝅥𝅯 𝅘𝅥𝅯 𝅘𝅥𝅯 𝅘𝅥𝅯 𝅘𝅥𝅯 𝅘𝅥𝅯	𝅘𝅥𝅰 𝅘𝅥𝅰 𝅘𝅥𝅰 𝅘𝅥𝅰 𝅘𝅥𝅰 𝅘𝅥𝅰 𝅘𝅥𝅰 𝅘𝅥𝅰 𝅘𝅥𝅰 𝅘𝅥𝅰 𝅘𝅥𝅰 𝅘𝅥𝅰

Writing Notes

The musical symbol system is written according to very specific rules. It is important that correct note-writing procedures be practiced from the beginning. While this presentation is not to be treated as a text for the writing of music manuscripts, a few important rules will be given. The interested student is referred to other sources for detailed information on writing music.*

   In Chapter 2, you will see that note heads are placed on lines or spaces appropriate to the pitch desired. For now, we will use a one-line staff to write rhythm-patterns, and we will use the **neutral clef**.† Notes written on the line are placed so that the line bisects the note head. The stem extends downward from the left side of the note when the note is above or on the line and extends upward from the right when the note head is below the line. These rules are illustrated in Example 1.9.

Example 1.9
Correct Note-Writing Procedure

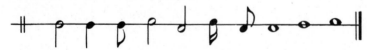

---

* See, for example, Gardner Read, *Music Notation* (Boston: Allyn and Bacon, 1969; reprinted by Crescendo Publishers, 132 W. 22nd Street, New York, N.Y. 10011).

† The neutral clef is a symbol used when there is no reference whatever to pitch, or when pitch differences are only approximate. It is generally used for indefinite-pitched percussion instruments.

When writing two or more eighth, sixteenth, or thirty-second notes, stems are often joined together by one, two, or three beams, respectively, instead of using separate flags. This procedure helps performers to read music more accurately, because the beam serves to highlight and group unit-patterns—notes which are to be played within one pulse. A recent innovation in notation suggests the placement of rests within the beamed units as illustrated in Example 1.10.

Example 1.10
Beaming Eighth, Sixteenth, and Thirty-Second Notes and Rests

Extended Duration

Duration of notes can be increased by two means. The first method is by the use of the **tie**. Any two notes representing the same pitch can be joined together by a curved line (a tie) to yield a sound of greater duration. The resulting duration is simply the sum of the two durations involved in the connection.

Example 1.11
The Function of the Tie

The second means of extending the duration of a note is by the addition of a dot immediately after the note (♩•). If the note head is on a line, the dot is placed above the line rather than on or below the line ♩•. The addition of a dot extends a note's duration by one-half its value. This procedure is summarized in Example 1.12.

Example 1.12
The Effect of the Durational Dot

NOTE	ASSIGNED* DURATION	DOTTED NOTE	DURATION OF DOT	TOTAL DURATION
♩	2 pulses	♩•	1 pulse	♩• = 3 pulses or
♩	1 pulse	♩•	½ pulse	♩• = 1½ pulses or
𝅝	4 pulses	𝅝•	2 pulses	𝅝• = 6 pulses or

* The notes shown do not always receive the number of pulses assigned here; the assigned durations simply serve to illustrate the principle involved.

On limited occasions a double dot can be used with notes, but composers have not chosen to make this a regular practice. When a double dot is used, the second dot increases note duration by one-half the value of the first dot. The following example illustrates how this works.

Example 1.13
The Effect of the Double Dot

NOTE	ASSIGNED VALUE	DOUBLE DOTTED NOTE	VALUE OF FIRST DOT	VALUE OF SECOND DOT	TOTAL DURATION
♩	2 pulses	♩••	1 pulse	½ pulse	♩•• = 3½ or ♩ ♩ ♪
♪	1 pulse	♪••	½ pulse	¼ pulse	♪•• = 1¾ or ♪ ♪ ♪

Rests are never tied; however, the duration of rests can be extended by the dot. This practice is limited and cannot be used indiscriminately.

_____
                                    (Name)

CHECK YOUR UNDERSTANDING
Chapter 1, No. 2

1. Symbols for musical sounds are called _____

2. Symbols for silence within a musical composition are called _____

3. Identify all parts of the note below.

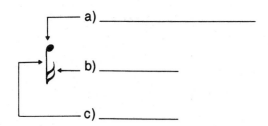
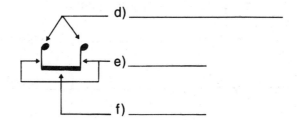

4. Name the following notes and rests.

    a) _____ 𝄾

    b) _____ 𝄾

    c) _____ 𝄿

    d) _____ 𝄾

    e) _____ 𝅗𝅥

5. Complete the following equivalents.

    a) 1 ♩ = 2 _____ notes.

    b) 2 ♩ = 8 _____ notes.

    c) 8 ♪ = 2 _____ notes.

    d) 4 ♬ = 1 _____ note.

    e) 4 𝅝 = 8 _____ notes.

25

6.   Match the following note and rest values.

a) 𝄽 _____   1. ▬

b) 𝅘𝅥𝅮 _____   2. 𝅘𝅥𝅮

c) ▬ _____   3. 𝄾

d) 𝅗𝅥 _____   4. 𝅘𝅥

e) 𝄾 _____   5. 𝅝

7.   Complete the following equivalents.

a) 2 𝄽 = 4 _____ rests.

b) 1 𝅗𝅥 = 8 _____ rests.

c) 6 𝄾 = 3 _____ rests.

d) 4 𝅘𝅥 = 2 _____ rests.

8.   Using the given values, fill in the missing durational values.

a) If 𝅘𝅥 has a value of 1 pulse then 𝅗𝅥 has a value of _____ pulse(s).

b) If 𝄾 has a value of 2 pulses then 𝄾 has a value of _____ pulse(s).

c) If 𝅘𝅥 has a value of ½ pulse then 𝅝 has a value of _____ pulse(s).

d) If 𝅗𝅥 has a value of 1 pulse then 𝅘𝅥𝅮 has a value of _____ pulse(s).

e) If 𝅘𝅥𝅮 has a value of 1 pulse then 𝅘𝅥 has a value of _____ pulse(s).

9.   Practice writing the following notes. Be sure to write some notes above and below the line.

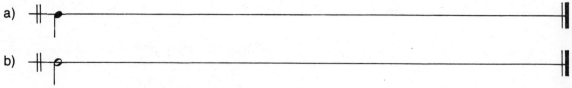

(continued)

(Name)

d)

e)

10.   Practice writing the following rests.

a)

b)

c)

d)

11.   Complete the following tie puzzles.

a) If ♩ receives 1 pulse, then 𝅝 ⌣ ♩ receives _____ pulse(s).

b) If ♪ receives 1 pulse, then ♩ ⌣ ♪ receives _____ pulse(s).

c) If ♩ receives 1 pulse, then ♪ ⌣ ♬ receives _____ pulse(s).

d) If ♪ receives 1 pulse, then ♪ ⌣ ♬ receives _____ pulse(s).

e) If ♩ receives 2 pulses, then ♩ ⌣ ♪ receives _____ pulse(s).

f) If 𝅝 receives 2 pulses, then 𝅝 ⌣ ♩ receives _____ pulse(s).

12.   Fill in the blanks below using two tied notes.

a) 𝅝 is equivalent to

b) ♩ is equivalent to

c) ♩. is equivalent to

d) ♩ is equivalent to

e) ♪ is equivalent to

13.   Fill in the blanks below with equivalent dotted notes.

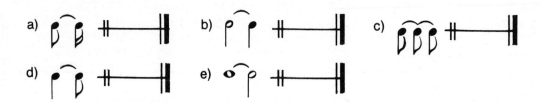

14.   Show the unit-patterns (using only regular division) of the given notes.

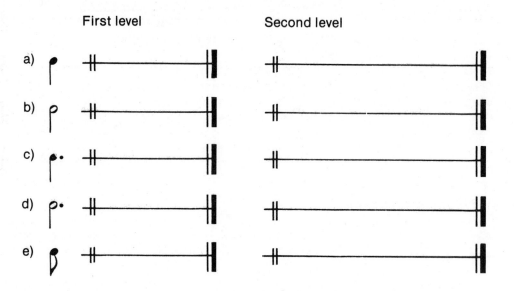

15.   Among the following, underscore only those terms or symbols that refer to *rhythm*.

note   rest   melody   dynamics   grace note   timbre
division   amplitude   dotted note   pulse   intensity
regular division   tempo   spectrum   unit   harmonic
unit-pattern   tie   rhythm-pattern   stem   beam
fundamental   dot   note value   loudness   frequency
pitch   double dot   flag   duration

(Be sure you can define all of the above.)

METER

Meter is a word of Greek origin and literally means "to measure." It is important to consider the concept of meter from two points of view: visual and aural. From the aural standpoint, we must consider the way in which pulses are grouped to form larger temporal units. Visually, we must consider the manner in which symbols are grouped to form both unit-patterns and **measures**.

Earlier in the chapter we saw how a listener tends to group fast, symmetrical sounds into pulses. In a similar manner, and at a higher level, the listener tends to group pulses into larger temporal units. This process tends to be guided by some real or imagined emphasis, or stress, applied to one of the pulses. As with the perception of pulse itself, the result of the perceptual pulse grouping can very easily be different for several listeners, since important aural clues may be interpreted differently.

Traditionally, certain beats have received stress according to a recurring scheme. At times, composers have chosen to adhere closely to these stress schemes. Frequently, however, composers deliberately mask or blot out these obvious patterns of stress in order to achieve greater musical interest. Suppose, for example, that the following series of pulses is performed without stress.

Example 1.14
Grouping of Pulses

Clearly, listeners have a large number of options regarding pulse grouping. The grouping perceived is most probably a result of environmental and cultural influences.

Turning from the aural to the visual aspect of meter, we find that music notation is organized into visually manageable segments by the use of lines drawn perpendicular to the staff. These lines, called **barlines**, do not have any durational value, nor do they indicate a pause or cessation in the musical flow.

Example 1.15
The Barline

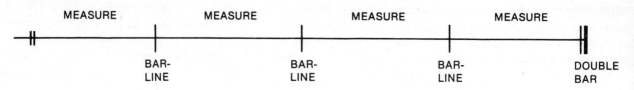

Double barlines occur in two forms: (a) two thin vertical lines to separate sections of a composition ——————————‖—————— and (b) one thin and one thicker vertical line to indicate the end of a composition or of one movement of a composition ——————————————‖.

As is shown in Example 1.15, the staff area between two barlines is called a **measure**. Each measure contains a specified amount of durational notation. This amount can change at designated points in a piece of music or it can remain constant throughout. Decisions regarding the total duration to be placed within measures are the composer's. The outcome of the composer's decision is communicated to the performer and other interested persons in the form of the **measure signature.***

Measure signatures are simply visual aids to performers and/or conductors, informing them how the written music will be divided into measures. A measure signature is found at the beginning of a piece of music and consists of two numerals arranged vertically on the staff. If for example the numerals $\frac{2}{4}$ appear at the beginning of a composition, the equivalent of two quarter notes will be contained in every measure. Many notational possibilities can fit a measure of $\frac{2}{4}$. A few are shown in Example 1.16. Close study will reveal that every measure contains the equivalent of two quarter notes.

Example 1.16
Sample Notation of $\frac{2}{4}$ "Skip to My Lou" (Folk)

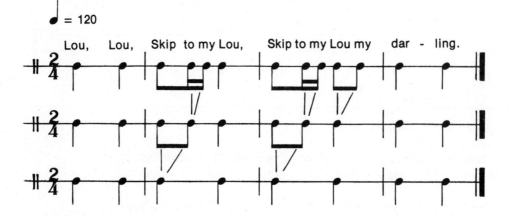

---

*   The measure signature is often called the "meter signature." We consider this term to be inaccurate because the signature does not necessarily designate the meter. The term "time signature," also frequently used, is vague because of the many ambiguous meanings of the word "time" in music.

Similarly, a measure signature of $\frac{5}{8}$ indicates that the equivalent of five eighth notes will be present in every measure. Again, many possible durational combinations can be placed in a single measure of $\frac{5}{8}$.

Example 1.17
Sample Notation of $\frac{5}{8}$ "Jarabe" (Mexican Folk Dance)

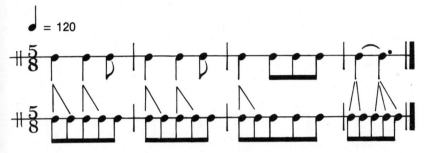

In theory, any numeral could be used as the upper number of a measure signature since the upper numeral indicates how many of a specific note (or its equivalent) will be contained in each measure. In practice, composers usually specify a number between 2 and 12 with an occasional extension to as high as 20* and a very rare appearance of 1. Study the following sample notation using the $\frac{6}{8}$ signature.

Example 1.18
Sample Notation of $\frac{6}{8}$ "One More River" (Spiritual)

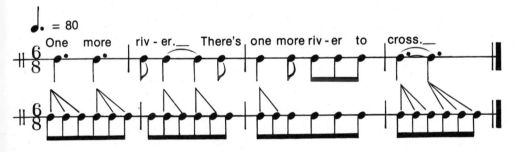

Lower numerals in measure signatures are restricted to those representing particular note values, all of them undotted notes, as indicated in Example 1.19. *There are no numerals that can be used to indicate dotted notes.* (However, as we shall see in the next section, contemporary composers have devised an alternative to the traditional measure signature that provides for this omission.)

---

*   The contemporary composer Elliot Carter, in his *String Quartet No. 1,* writes with a signature of $\frac{21}{8}$.

Example 1.19
Lower Numeral Representation of Durational Note Values

NUMERAL	NOTE REPRESENTED
1	𝅝
2	𝅗𝅥
4	♩
8	♪
16	𝅘𝅥𝅯
32	𝅘𝅥𝅰

CHECK YOUR UNDERSTANDING

Chapter 1, No. 3

1. How many measures are there in the following? _____

2. Where are double bars used in music notation? _____

_____

_____

_____

3. Indicate the meaning of the following measure signatures.

    a) $\frac{2}{8}$ _____

    b) $\frac{3}{4}$ _____

    c) $\frac{9}{8}$ _____

    d) $\frac{6}{4}$ _____

    e) $\frac{7}{8}$ _____

4. Supply an appropriate measure signature after the neutral clef sign in the
    following. (There are several possibilities.) Perform each by chanting on a
    neutral syllable such as "tah." Be careful to sustain sound duration as notated.

    a)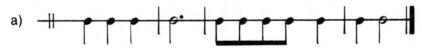

    b)

    c)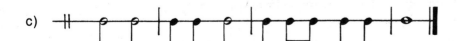

    d)

5.   Place barlines in the appropriate places in the following notation. Perform each by chanting on a neutral syllable such as "tah." Be careful to sustain sound duration as notated.

a)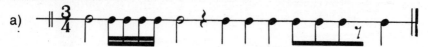

b)

c)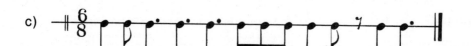

d)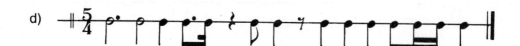

e)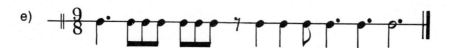

6.   Fill in each measure using a single note or rest symbol to make it complete according to the measure signature.

a)    b)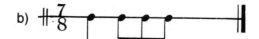

c)    d)

e)    a)

g)    h)

i)    j)

7.   Among the following, underscore only those terms or symbols that refer to *meter.*

measure   pulse   intensity   barline   fundamental

measure signature $\frac{2}{4}$ note   neutral clef sign

(Be sure you can define all of the above.)

MOTION

The **motion** of musical sounds through time is controlled by assigning specific time lengths to durational notation. This process is accomplished by awarding the value of one pulse to a specific, single note. This note, since it represents one beat, is the basic unit of musical flow for the composition.

Any note, dotted or undotted, can visually represent a single pulse. The choice of which note will represent one pulse is entirely up to the composer. As in the case of the measure signature, at any point changes can take place within a composition which warrant selecting a different note to represent a single pulse.

Musical flow is communicated visually by the conductor to ensemble performers and the audience through the use of **conducting patterns.** These patterns represent the number of pulses per measure only, and in no way indicate any specific note values. A grouping of four pulses per measure is indicated by the same visual pattern regardless of whether eighth, quarter, dotted quarter, or half notes are the units of beat. The basic conducting patterns are illustrated in Example 1.20.

Example 1.20
The Traditional Conducting Patterns

2 BEATS PER MEASURE	3 BEATS PER MEASURE	4 BEATS PER MEASURE	5 BEATS PER MEASURE

6 BEATS PER MEASURE	7 BEATS PER MEASURE	9 BEATS PER MEASURE

The diagrams in Example 1.20 are the view as seen by the conductor. Although these are, in outline, the basic patterns, conductors often vary from them.

Composers indicate the pulse and the unit of beat in several ways. Often the measure signature indicates which note will be the unit. The lower numeral *can* carry this information, but composers usually rely on a tempo indication to clarify the unit designation. Also, the grouping of notes into unit-patterns is sometimes a clue to meter.

To illustrate how tempo indication affects the selecting of the unit of beat, suppose a composer chooses $\frac{2}{4}$ and indicates a tempo of ♪ = 60. Then the performer or conductor is aware that the eighth note will serve as the unit of beat and that the felt pulse of the music will be represented by the eighth note. The conductor will therefore conduct in a pattern of four pulses per measure.* Various conducting gestures could be used, for example, a 4 pattern or a divided 2. In rare instances, a $\frac{2}{4}$ signature may move along at a very fast tempo with the half note as the unit. In such an instance, the tempo indication would perhaps be ♩ = 92. The conductor would then conduct in a pattern of one pulse per measure.

If, on the other hand, no indication of tempo is given with the $\frac{2}{4}$ signature, most performers and conductors will—for better or worse—assume the quarter note to be the unit and proceed accordingly. Unfortunately, some composers are careless about indicating tempo. Often the necessary information, if present, is given only approximately, as by use of the term "moderately" or the Italian equivalent *moderato*. The most desirable tempo instruction is a precise metronomic indication, such as ♩ = 84. This exact tempo information is essential if performers and conductors are to interpret the music precisely.

Another example will help to illustrate the interrelatedness of tempo, meter, and unit. The measure signature $\frac{6}{8}$ indicates that every measure will contain the equivalent of six eighth notes. Without any indication of tempo, it is unclear which note will serve as the unit of beat. If tempo is indicated as ♪ = 72, then the eighth note is clearly the unit representation of a single pulse. Such a designation would result in six pulses per measure, and the conductor would conduct in a pattern of six beats per measure. If the composer indicated ♩. = 120, the conductor or performer would organize on the basis of two pulses in a measure. The latter course is the usual solution to a signature of $\frac{6}{8}$. In rare instances, the composer may indicate ♩. = 96. The performer would then solve rhythmic problems on the basis of one pulse per measure, the dotted half note being the unit of beat.

Many present-day composers substitute a *note* for the lower numeral of the measure signature. A $\frac{6}{8}$ signature with an eighth-note pulse in a moderate tempo would be indicated $\frac{6}{♪}$. At a fast tempo the signature would be indicated $\frac{2}{♩.}$, with the dotted quarter note receiving the beat in a two-pulse measure.

The importance of the tempo plus the information contained in the measure signature becomes clear when the performer is asked to perform intricate rhythm-patterns. It is only by first identifying the unit that performers can solve rhythmic

---

*   It might have been advisable, in this instance, for the composer to have used a measure signature of $\frac{4}{8}$.

reading problems through the various counting systems employed. The ability to function equally well with all types of unit designations is necessary to understand musical time. The information regarding unit designation, pulse, and tempo is summarized in Example 1.21, for measure signatures in which the quarter note is the apparent unit. As the example shows, actual units depend on the tempo. Similar tabular forms could be developed for measure signatures that appear to be based on eighth, half, sixteenth, and thirty-second note units.

Example 1.21
Meter, Unit, and Tempo

MEASURE SIGNATURE		MODERATE TEMPO	VERY SLOW TEMPO	VERY FAST TEMPO
2/4	Pulses	2	4	1
	Unit	♩	♪	♩
3/4	Pulses	3	6	1
	Unit	♩	♪	♩.
* C 4/4	Pulses	4	8	2 * ¢
	Unit	♩	♪	♩
5/4	Pulses	5	10	2 ¦ 2
	Unit	♩	♪	♩ ♩. ¦ ♩. ♩
6/4	Pulses	6	12	2
	Unit	♩	♪	♩.
7/4	Pulses	7	14	3 ¦ 3 ¦ 3
	Unit	♩	♪	♩ ♩ ♩. ¦ ♩ ♩. ♩ ¦ ♩. ♩ ♩
8/4	Pulses	8	16	3 ¦ 3 ¦ 3
	Unit	♩	♪	♩. ♩. ♩ ¦ ♩. ♩ ♩. ¦ ♩ ♩. ♩.
9/4	Pulses	9	18	3
	Unit	♩	♪	♩.

---

*   C = 4/4. At a faster tempo, when there are two pulses per measure, a line is drawn through the C (¢) resulting in 2/2 or alla breve.

STAFF FOR SKETCHING

CHECK YOUR UNDERSTANDING

Chapter 1, No. 4

1. What factors will the performer and/or conductor use to determine which note will serve as a unit of pulse?

    _____

    _____

    _____

2. Describe, in your own words, the meaning of the term *unit of beat.*

    _____

    _____

3. What kinds of musical notes can serve as units of beat?

    _____

4. If a quarter note is designated as one unit of beat, what values are assigned to the following notes and rests?

    a) 𝄽 _____   b) ▬ _____   c) ▬ _____

    d) 𝄾 _____   e) 𝄾 _____   f) ♬ _____

    g) ♩. _____   h) 𝅗𝅥. _____   i) ♪ _____

5. What is the unit of beat for each of the following examples?

    _____ a)

    _____ b)

    _____ c)

    _____ d)

39

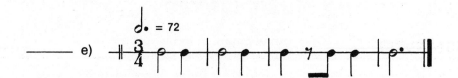

6.   Insert the appropriate measure signature in each of the following.

7.   Among the following, underscore only those terms or symbols that refer to *rhythm.*

unit   timbre   conducting pattern   beam   amplitude
measure   harmonics   tempo   unit of beat

(Be sure you can define all of the above.)

Activities for Developing Music Literacy

These suggested activities are designed for class, small group, or individual use in developing your aural skill. In some cases, instructors or designated students may dictate exercises for notational response by the others. In other cases, you may find it beneficial to work individually or in pairs. The more time you spend on these activities, the easier it will be to convert sounds to written symbols, or written symbols to sounds. But the mental process must be an active part of these activities, because thinking in terms of music sound requires a firm grounding in fundamental music knowledge.

AURAL AND KEYBOARD DRILL

In this activity you will focus on converting the written symbols of music into sounds (music reading) and on converting sounds into music symbols (melodic, harmonic, and rhythmic **dictation**). You can develop your ability by singing and by instrumental playing, but probably most of all through directed drills at the piano keyboard. No keyboard drills are included in this chapter but many are provided in Chapters 2-5.

1. Practice imagining a tempo of one beat per second (60 per minute). Double this speed to achieve 120. Triple it to achieve 180. Divide the 180 in half to reach 90. Practice conducting patterns in two, three, four, five, and six beats per measure in all these tempos. Try to fix the various tempo rates clearly in your memory.

2. Practice conducting groups of two, three, four, five, and six beats. Include both periodic and nonperiodic beats. Accurate beats can be better attained if you think and feel first level division while conducting in two, three, or four. (See small numerals above notes.)

Models (*Periodic*)

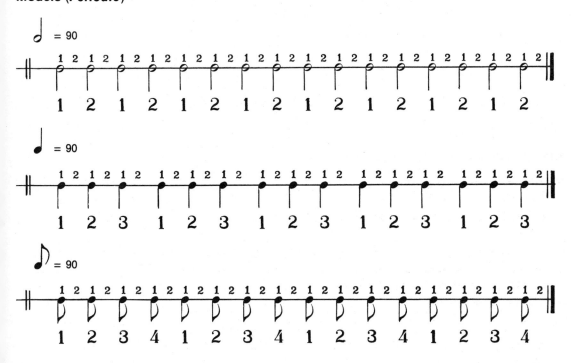

Models (*Nonperiodic*)

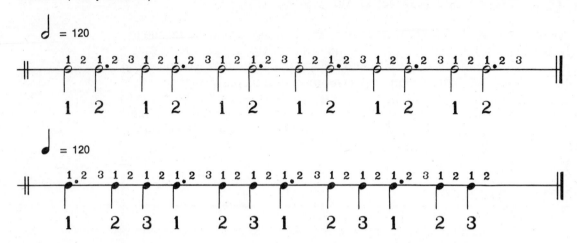

3.   Work with another student to perform twelve periodic beat sounds using the neutral syllables "tah" and "lah." Use conducting patterns to indicate a variety of beat groupings. Use "tah" on the first beat of each group and "lah" for the remaining beats. The natural recurrence of emphasis resulting from syllable change will aid in identifying beat groups.

Models

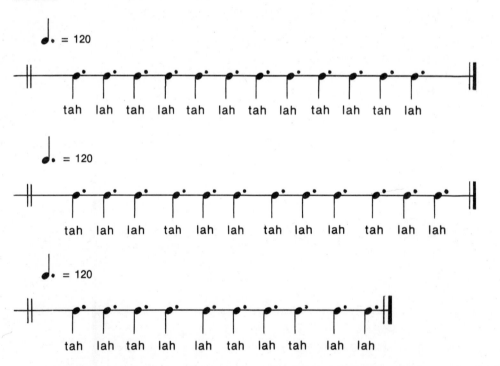

4.   To gain facility in pulse division, practice the following. Have different students participate in each group. Perform at different tempos. Use different vocal sounds (tah, tee, tay, too) or body sounds (clap, snap, stamp, thigh slap). Repeat as desired.

Models

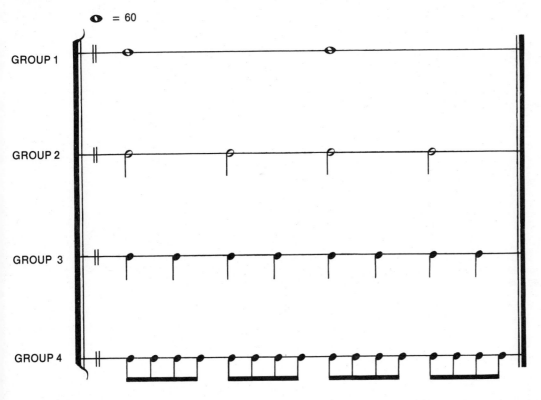

Change parts and repeat this drill. Use different note values, either dotted or undotted. Nonpitched percussion instruments may also be used.

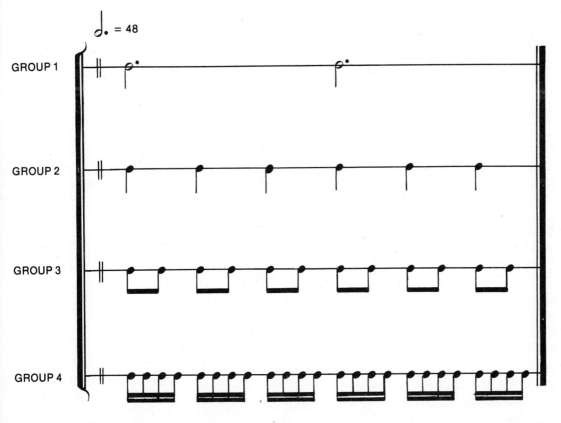

5.   In class or in small groups, move around the room stepping and clapping. Step a pulse and clap its division.

Models

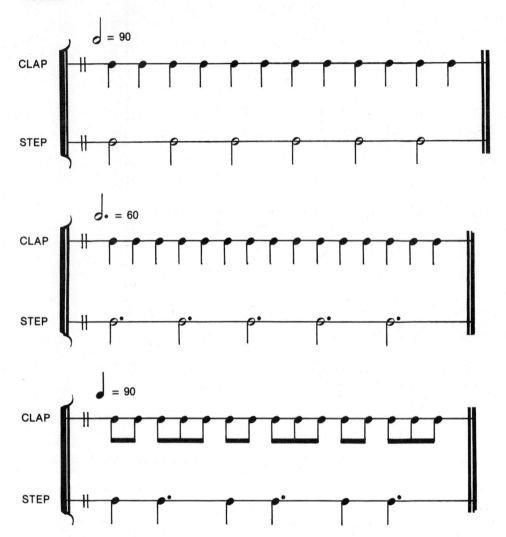

Invent different exercises of your own. Use different tempos and perhaps add a third motion, such as a "head nod" to provide a further division of pulse.*

---

*   These approaches to developing rhythm as a feeling of motion through body motion (**eurhythmics**) are the views proposed by Emile Jacques-Dalcroze in *Rhythm, Music and Education* (New York: G. P. Putnam's Sons, 1925). Many other variations and adaptations of movement to the development of rhythmic feeling are possible.

Model

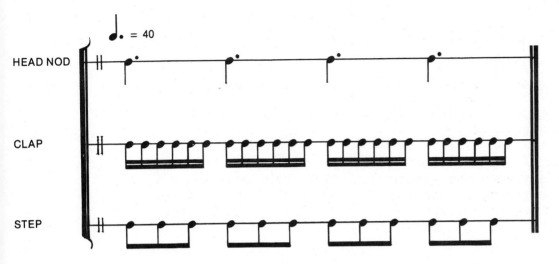

6.   Given a tempo set by the instructor (or a designated student), count beats
during a period of silence.

Model

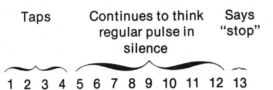

The instructor establishes the tempo by tapping and counting the first four
beats. Continue to count beats silently until told to stop. Repeat this exercise
using a variety of tempos and both periodic and nonperiodic beats. Check for
accuracy. (A silent, blinking metronome can be used by instructor.)

7.   The instructor dictates a series of pulse sounds, indicating various beat groupings by stress. Notate these using a ♩ to represent each pulse sound. As an aid
for hearing beat groups, think the number one (1) on each stressed beat, such
as 1 2 3 1 2 3. Draw barlines between beat groups. Vary the number of
sounds in each grouping.

Models

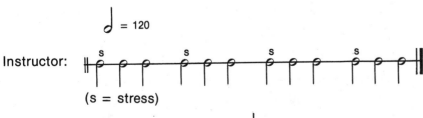

Student: Notate on one-line staff with ♩ representing pulse.

Instructor:

Student: Notate on one-line staff with ♩. and ♩ representing pulse.

> (The person dictating must think division of the pulse in order to maintain a steady tempo.)

8. The instructor dictates a series of nonstressed pulse sounds. Conduct to the pulse using a conducting pattern of two (2). Start at a pace of 60 and gradually increase the tempo. As the tempo increases, conduct first to every sound, second to every other sound, third to every third sound, fourth to every fourth sound.

Model

Sounds: ●   ●   ●   ●   ●   ● ● ● ● ● ● ● ● ● ●

Beats: | | | | | | | | | |

Sounds: ● ● ● ● ● ● ● ● ● ● ● ● ● ● ●●●●●●●●●●●●●●●●●●●●

Beats: | | | | | | | | | |

> Repeat the exercise using the same approach but keep time through motion. For example, clap the pulse sounds and step, first to each pulse sound, then to every other sound, and so forth.

9. The instructor dictates a series of rhythmic events, using pulses, division (first level unit-patterns), ties between pulses, and rests. Write the dictated pattern.

Models

Instructor plays and student writes:

♩ = 90

Instructor plays and student writes:

♩. = 60

10. The instructor writes short rhythmic events on the chalkboard or overhead projector, then taps the rhythms with a purposely performed error. Check the pulse number where the error occurred.

Models

Written: Performed:

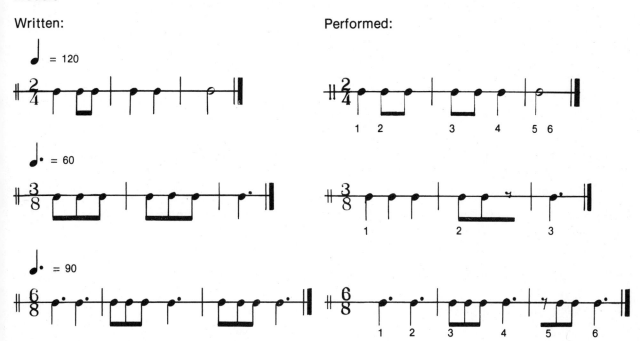

ANALYTICAL LISTENING

Listening activity is generally associated with music appreciation classes where the study of music sometimes neglects the structure of music. Further, jazz, rock, pop, and folk music are usually omitted. But analytical study of all music will help solidify important concepts in each of the chapters in this book. This study will also make you a more perceptive musician. Listening to music should be given focus by analyzing its basic parameters. In this chapter our interest is primarily in rhythm, with special emphasis on beat and division.

Listen to and conduct the following musical selections. Where possible obtain the score and analyze the aspects of the rhythm parameter noted.

1. Armstrong, "Struttin' With Some Barbecue," *Smithsonian Collection of Classic Jazz,* performed by Louis Armstrong and His Hot Five, P 11892.
Pulse, particularly during the improvised chorus of Louis Armstrong.

2. Beethoven, *Symphony No. 7 in A Major,* Movement II, Theme 1. Performed by the NBC Symphony Orchestra conducted by Arturo Toscanini, RCA Victor LM1756.
Pulse and division.

3. Brown and Fain, "That Old Feeling," in *Waiter, Make Mine Blues.* Performed by Anita O'Day, Verve MG V 2145.
Pulse, particularly in the first chorus with voice and acoustic bass only.

4.   Copland, *Billy the Kid,* Scene 1, Theme 3. Performed by the New York Philharmonic conducted by Leonard Bernstein, Columbia MS 6175.
      Nonperiodic pulse.

5.   Grainger, "No. 2 Horkstrow Grange," *The Lincolnshire Posy.* Performed by the Eastman Wind Ensemble conducted by Frederick Fennel, Mercury Records MG 50173.
      Pulse.

6.   Handel, *Water Music Suite No. 2 in D,* Movement V, "Minuet." Performed by The Hague Philharmonic conducted by Pierre Boulez, Nonesuch Records H71127.
      Pulse.

7.   Haydn, *Symphony No. 94 in G,* Movement II, Theme 1. Performed by Berlin Philharmonic conducted by Karl Richter, Deutsche Grammophon Gesellschaft 138782 SCPM.
      Pulse and division.

8.   Lennon and McCartney, "Hey Jude." Performed by The Beatles, Apple Records 2276.
      Pulse.

9.   Nyro, "And When I Die." Performed by Blood Sweat and Tears, Columbia Records 445008.
      Pulse, division, grouping, tempo.

10.   Raskin, "Those Were the Days." Performed by Mary Hopkins, Apple Records 1801.
      Pulse and division.

IMPROVISATION

Improvisation is the spontaneous expression of musical ideas through performance. The testing of materials through improvisation helps to develop aural skill and competence. It also stimulates the creative process.

1.   Improvise on a time line using either periodic or nonperiodic pulse. (A time line is simply a line drawn on the chalkboard to represent motion from the beginning to the end of a musical happening.) After dividing the line into pulses, use various vocal sounds, nonsense syllables, or body sounds to create a musical event. The instructor follows the time line with finger moving from left to right. To begin, make the sounds coincident with pulses or equal to tied pulses. Repeat this activity, but be sure to draw a new time line on each occasion.

Models

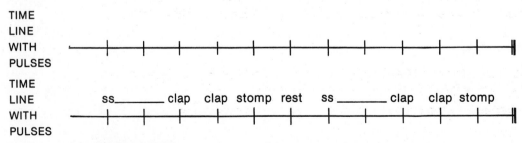

TIME LINE WITH PULSES

TIME LINE WITH PULSES

ss = hissing sound

2.   Divide the class in two or more groups as needed. Choose one-syllable words (tree, foot, man, peach). Set a pulse and maintain a repetitive verbal chant.

Model

Pulse: tree   tree   tree   tree   tree   tree   tree   tree   tree

Using division achieved by two-syllable words (hem-lock, inch-es, wo-man, ap-ple), create a musical event. Be sure to use rests to create added interest.

Model

Division: hem-lock   hem-lock   hem-lock   hem-lock   hem-lock
Pulse: tree   tree   tree   tree   tree

Other words may be used to create different levels of division, such as by three or four.

Models

Division: bob-o-link   ro-de-o   blue-ber-ry
Pulse: tree   tree   tree

Division: mo-tor-cy-cle   par-a-troo-per   huck-le-ber-ry
Pulse: tree   tree   tree

3.   Using a variety of vocal sounds of varying pitch, such as crying, wailing, moaning, cheek popping, hissing, tongue clacking, throat clearing, humming, "r" rolling, and lip buzzing, create a musical event lasting 30-60 seconds. Pulse can be of equal or unequal length but the grouping of pulses (if unequal) should be regular (long, short, long, short, etc.). Use pulses, first and/or second level divisions, ties between pulses, and rests. The class or small group could be divided as follows.

Model

GROUP 1	GROUP 2	GROUP 3
hiss	bomp, bomp	ta-ka, ta-ka
	(low pitch)	(high pitch)
(loud)	(soft)	(soft)

A score for this type of improvisation is shown below.

♩ = 60

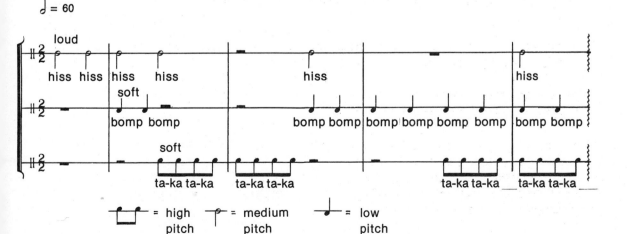

4.   Decide upon a series of sounds lasting about 10 seconds. Use pulses, divisions, ties between pulses, and rests. After memorizing the series divide the class into three sections. Have each group perform the series but use a staggered start. This will produce a music composition known as a **canon**.

Model

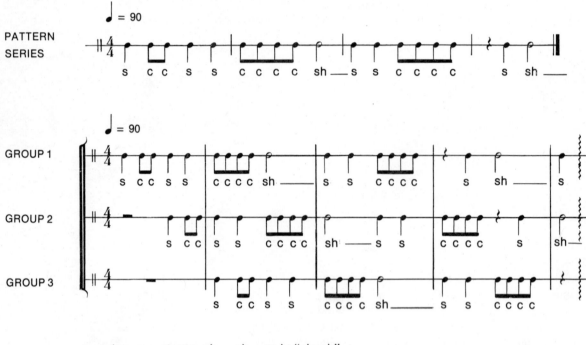

c = clap, s = stomp, sh = sh— as in "shush"

Try having Groups 2 and 3 enter on beats other than the above. Percussion instruments may also be used.

CREATIVE WRITING

Creative writing is the forming of music ideas (often encountered through improvisation) into organized, written symbols in a format ready for performance. This activity is not one designed exclusively for the composer, for the understanding of the way music is put together is of great significance to the performer (the re-creator) and the listener.

1.   Prepare a time line of 24 pulses for presentation and performance. Be careful to notate accurately. (See model given under Improvisation 1.)

2.   Notate accurately an event similar to Improvisation 2. Choose words for chanting or perhaps different percussion instruments.

3.   Compose a rhythmic composition similar to Improvisation 2. Carefully complete the score, using a one-line staff for each part. Write in the vocal sounds and indicate which parts are to be played loud or soft. Each group could use more than one sound, which you will, of course, notate. Again, percussion instruments may be used in place of chanting.

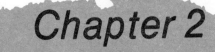

Harmony

The Notation of Pitch; Alteration Signs;
Naming the Octaves; Clefs and Staffs; Intervals;
Inversion of Intervals; Triads

In Chapter 1 we made no attempt to present notes as symbols for the designation of pitch, although we did present various kinds of notes as symbols of duration. We are now ready to introduce the subject of pitch notation in a systematic way. In the process, we shall briefly cover the history of pitch notation, to show how musicians have arrived at their present-day notation, which enables them to specify a large vocabulary of pitches by written symbols.

THE NOTATION OF PITCH

Our starting point in notating pitch will be a tone vibrating at the frequency of 440 Hz: A.* Other pitches used in music are mathematically related to this tone in a way dependent upon the system of tuning being employed. Today, most professional instruments of the world are tuned according to a system known as **equal temperament**—a system which divides the perfect octave† into twelve different and equally spaced pitches. The first seven letters of the alphabet (A, B, C, D, E, F, G) are used to designate these twelve pitches as well as those repeated at the octaves higher or lower.

In order to understand how seven letters can designate twelve pitches it is helpful to refer to the construction of the piano keyboard. A small section of the keyboard is pictured in Example 2.1.

Example 2.1
The Piano Keyboard

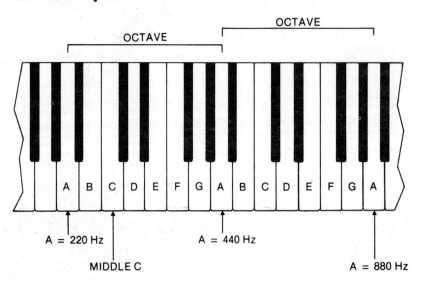

Example 2.1 identifies seven different pitches within an octave (A, B, C, D, E, F, G) and, of course their duplication at the octave. These seven pitches are all produced on the white keys‡ of the piano keyboard. They are usually referred to as the **basic scale** and are used to construct the seven basic **diatonic scales** discussed in Chapter 3.

---

*   Tuners sometimes vary slightly from this norm.

†   A perfect octave is the name of the **interval** in which the ratio of vibrations is 1:2. (When we speak of "the octave," we are usually referring to the "perfect octave.") An octave above A = 440 vibrates 880 times per second and is also labelled A. An octave below A = 440 is A = 220; A = 880 is two octaves above A = 220. All of these A's are members of the A **pitch class**.

‡   The black and white colors are usually reversed on the harpsichord keyboard.

Between the pitches produced by these white keys are **melodic intervals** (pitch differences between two successive tones) of both **half steps** and **whole steps.** A half step is exactly 1/12 of the octave and is the smallest pitch interval in our present-day, equal-tempered scale system of tuning. A whole step is 1/6 of the octave and is equal to two half steps. The half- and whole-step arrangement of the white keys is shown in Example 2.2.

Example 2.2
The Half- and Whole-Step Arrangement of the White Keys

```
                    OCTAVE
    ┌─────────────────────────────────┐
 A    B C    D    E F    G      A

        └─┘        └─┘
   1   ½   1    1   ½   1     1
```

In this example only one octave is shown, with the first A repeated an octave higher. The point to remember is that **half steps occur only between B and C and between E and F.**

The remaining five pitches within the octave (so far we have labelled only seven) are produced by the five black keys. These supply the needed half-step intervals between the white keys A and B, C and D, D and E, F and G, and G and A, as shown in Example 2.3.

Example 2.3
The Twelve Divisions of the Octave (Keyboard)

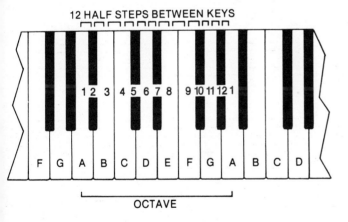

We have now identified on the keyboard the twelve pitches in the octave. If they are played in consecutive order they produce a **chromatic scale.** If they are played simultaneously they produce an octave **tone cluster.**

STAFF FOR SKETCHING

CHECK YOUR UNDERSTANDING

Chapter 2, No. 1

1. A perfect octave is the name of the interval in which the ratio of vibrations is

   _____ : _____ .

2. If middle C is tuned to vibrate at 262 times per second, the C an octave higher

   would vibrate at _____ times per second, and the C an octave lower than

   middle C would vibrate at _____ times per second.

3. In today's tuning system there are _____ pitches within the octave.

4. List the seven letters of the alphabet used to designate the white keys on the

   piano: _____ _____ _____ _____ _____ _____ _____

5. On the piano keyboard groups of _____ black keys alternate with groups of

   _____ black keys.

6. Name the pitches produced by playing the white keys below. (Write on the
   diagram.)

7. A half step is what part of an octave? _____

8. A whole step is what part of an octave? _____

9. With reference to white keys only, half steps occur between _____ and _____

   and between _____ and _____ .

10. With reference to white keys only, whole steps occur between _____ and

    _____ , between _____ and _____ , between _____ and _____ ,

    between _____ and _____ , and between _____ and _____ .

11. Not counting octave duplications, how many pitches are produced by the white

    keys? _____

12.   The black keys create the needed half steps between _____ and _____, between _____ and _____, between _____ and _____, between _____ and _____, and between _____ and _____.

13.   If all keys shown in Question 6 were played in consecutive order (starting on on the first key to the left), the result would be a _____ scale.

14.   Among the following, underscore only those terms or symbols that refer to the *notation of pitch.*

equal temperament   pulse   frequency   octave   meter
bar   measure   Hz   scale   interval   tempo   half step
middle C   A = 440   tone cluster   chromatic scale

(Be sure you can define all of the above.)

ALTERATION SIGNS

The naming of the black keys may be somewhat confusing to the beginner. The confusion results from the need for two or even three names. For now, certain statements must be accepted at face value. Later, when we turn to the study of scales and **tonality**, we can clarify the rationale for using different names.

Let us consider only two consecutive white-key pitches C and D and the pitch produced by the intervening black key. (Refer to Example 2.3.) This black key is called either C-sharp (a half step above C) or D-flat (a half step below D), depending upon how the tone functions in music. For clarity, the C and the D are sometimes called C-natural and D-natural. The following **alteration signs** are used: ♮ = **natural**; ♯ = **sharp**; and ♭ = **flat**. In some instances a **double sharp** (✕) and a **double flat** (♭♭) are required to notate music correctly. Example 2.4 illustrates how the five alteration signs affect the pitch C. Notice that C♭♭ is one half step lower in pitch than C♭; C is one half step lower than C♮; C♯ is one half step higher than C♮; etc.*

Example 2.4
Alteration Signs

←— Descending in pitch by half step increments
Ascending in pitch by half step increments —→

C♭♭		C♭		C♮		C♯		C✕
	½		½		½		½	

Observe that the letter names in Example 2.4 actually identify five different pitches, each a half step apart. Notice, also, that the use of alteration signs (♯, ♭, etc.) can produce a single pitch that has more than one name. The vertically aligned spellings in Example 2.5 represent identical pitches.

Example 2.5
Multiple Spellings (Enharmonics)

				E♭♭
		D♭♭	D♭	D♮
C♭♭	C♭	C♮	C♯	C✕
B♭	B♮	B♯	B✕	
A♯	A✕			

As the example indicates, when a single pitch is spelled in two or more ways (for example, C♯ and D♭) the pitches are said to be **enharmonic** with each other. In practice, double sharps and double flats are relatively less common than the other alteration signs, because composers can usually find ways of avoiding their use. Therefore, although you must be able to recognize both these signs and understand

---

*   In staff notation, alteration signs are always placed on the correct line or space directly *before* the note they alter. For correct drawings of symbols and their placement refer to Gardner Read, *Music Notation* (Boston: Allyn and Bacon, 1969; reprinted by Crescendo Publishers, 132 W. 22nd Street, New York, N. Y. 10011).

their function, we need not dwell on them further. With double flats and double sharps omitted, the enharmonics are as shown in Example 2.6.

Example 2.6
Enharmonic Equivalents

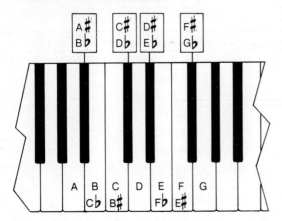

_____

(Name)

CHECK YOUR UNDERSTANDING

Chapter 2, No. 2

1. Supply correct name for each of the following symbols.

   a) ♮ _____

   b) ♯ _____

   c) ♭ _____

   d) 𝄪 _____

   e) ♭♭ _____

2. The above symbols are called _____ _____ .

3. a) A _____ raises the pitch of a natural tone (♮) by a half step.

   b) A _____ lowers the pitch of a natural tone (♮) by a half step.

   c) A _____ lowers the pitch of a sharped tone (♯) by a half step.

   d) A _____ raises the pitch of a flatted tone (♭) by a half step.

4. Place the following scrambled symbols in consecutive order from lowest to highest pitch with the lowest on the left: (D♮ D♭♭ D♯ D𝄪 D♭).

   _____ _____ _____ _____ _____

5. In your solution to Question 4, the distance between consecutive pitches is a _____ _____ in each instance.

6. There are _____ half steps between D♭ and D♯, and _____ half steps between D♭♭ and D𝄪.

7. Notice that in referring to pitch by letter names (D♯, for example) the alteration sign is placed *after* the letter. In music notation, however, alteration signs are always placed _____ the note.

8. Draw ten or more of each alteration sign, copying the models as nearly as possible. Use ink.

   —♮——————————————————————————————————

   ————————————————————————————————————

   —♯——————————————————————————————————

   ————————————————————————————————————

   —♭——————————————————————————————————

   ————————————————————————————————————

9.   In the boxes, write two possible names for each of the pitches indicated.

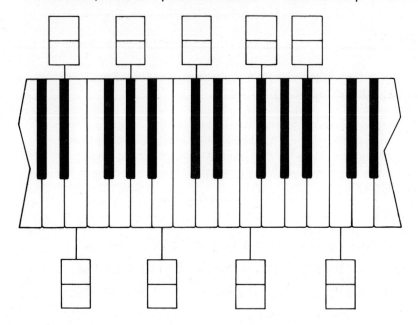

10.   Pitches which sound the same but are labelled differently (for example, C♯ and Db) are said to be _____ with each other.

11.   Supply an enharmonic for each of the given pitches.

a) D♯ _____   b) Eb _____   c) Gb _____

d) A♯ _____   e) Ab _____   f) G♯ _____

g) B♯ _____   h) C _____   i) Fb _____

j) Bb _____   k) Cb _____   l) Db _____

m) C✕ _____   n) D _____   o) Ebb _____

p) F✕ _____   q) E♯ _____   r) Bbb _____

12.   Among the following, underscore only those terms or symbols that refer specifically to *alteration signs.*

sharp   db   natural   octave   double bar   double flat
enharmonic spelling   meter   double sharp   neutral clef

(Be sure you can define all of the above.)

NAMING THE OCTAVES

All of the pitches within any octave have now been named. The keys on the piano du-plicate these pitches at various octaves to supply a range of over seven octaves—88 pitches. Almost all of the music we hear, whether from voices or from band and or-chestral instruments, falls within these extremes.

Example 2.7 (on the next page) pictures the entire piano keyboard, along with the attendant **grand staff**, to be explained shortly. The white keys are identified accord-ing to a system proposed by the Acoustical Society of America—a simple and direct system that has special advantages today because it is more applicable to computer programming than are other systems.*

---

*   The following system of naming the octaves (from low to high pitches) is also in common use. The lowest pitches are called subcontra A and B (denoted AAA and BBB). The lowest full octave from C through B is called the contra octave (CC, DD, etc.), and the re-maining octaves, in order, are called the large octave (C), the small octave (c), the one-line octave (c1 or c̄), the two-line octave (c2 or c̄), the three-line octave (c3 or c̄), and the four-line octave (c4 or c̄). The final key is called five-line C (c5 or c̄).

Example 2.7
The Piano Keyboard and the Grand Staff (Naming the Octaves)

MIDDLE C

CHECK YOUR UNDERSTANDING

Chapter 2, No. 3

Notice in Example 2.7 that the pitches from middle C up to and including the next B are referred to as C4, D4, E4, F4, G4, A4, and B4. Also, C♯4, D♭4, D♯4, E♭4, F♯4, etc., are so labelled. The octave designation always changes (when ascending) at the note C. By following this plan and referring to Example 2.7 as needed, identify the designated keys in the figure with correct octave labelling.

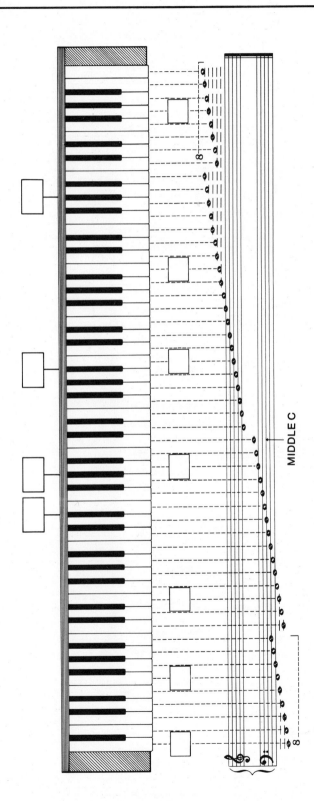

STAFF FOR SKETCHING

CLEFS AND STAFFS

Although we have identified by their letter names all the pitches on the piano keyboard, we have not explained the procedure for producing the staff notation that is
shown in Example 2.7.

Three basic elements are required for staff notation of pitch:

1. A symbol which will indicate duration as well as pitch. This symbol, the **note**,
    was presented in Chapter 1.

2. A music **staff,** ≡≡≡≡≡≡≡, on which the notes will be placed.

3. A **clef sign**, which when properly placed on the staff identifies a specific pitch.
    The following clef signs identify G4, C4, and F3.

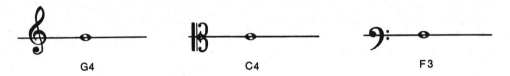

G4   C4   F3

In theory, pitches could be notated only by the use of the letters A, B, C, D, E, F,
G, along with the alteration signs A♯, B♭, etc,; however, this procedure would not
by itself show the duration of tones. To overcome this problem, notes of the desired
durational values are placed on staff lines or spaces which represent specific pitches.
For purposes of identification the staff lines and spaces are numbered as follows.

LINES   3 4 5 / 2 1 ≡≡≡≡≡≡≡ 4 3 / 1 2   SPACES

To see how the conventions of staff notation have developed, let us look at one
of the earlier staffs in the history of notation, a two-line staff.

Example 2.8
Two-Line Staff

In Example 2.8, the notes represent four adjacent **ascending*** pitches on the
keyboard's white keys. Adjacent notes (A, B, C, D, E, F, G, A, B, C,etc.) are placed on
line, space, line, space, etc., with ascending notes corresponding to ascending
(higher) pitches. Observe, however, that although we know the rhythm in Example 2.8,
we do not know the pitches. The four notes could represent A, B, C, and D, or they

---

*   A series of successively higher pitches is said to be **ascending**. This corresponds to
movement from left to right on the piano keyboard. A **descending** pitch series is characterized by
successively lower pitches, or right-to-left motion on the piano keyboard.

could represent B, C, D, and E, or C, D, E, and F, or D, F, A, and G, etc. It is necessary, then, for us to specify one line or one space as having a particular pitch which can be used as a starting point. If we place the letter C on the lower line (before the measure signature) to identify middle C, the example becomes quite specific in terms of both pitch and rhythm.

Example 2.9
Staff Identification

In the history of music notation the letter C as a symbol for identifying middle C became stylized and was eventually transformed into a more ornate **C clef**, which is used to a great extent today for music written for violas, cellos, and often bassoons and trombones. The usual form is as follows.

Middle C is notated on the line.

The problem with using a two-line staff is, of course, that it provides for only four or five pitches. The range of pitches can be increased somewhat by using short horizontal extension lines, called **ledger lines**, for higher or lower pitches. This device is illustrated in Example 2.10. (Can you name the tune?)

Example 2.10
Ledger Lines

However, for reasons that will soon become clear, it made more sense to simply increase the number of lines in the staff itself. The staff in past centuries varied from one line to as many as fifteen lines, finally standardizing at five lines (except for the grand staff, which is actually a combination of two staffs).

Example 2.11 shows the musical fragment in Example 2.10 as it would be written on a five-line staff with the C clef placed on the middle, or third, line. When placed here, the clef that identifies middle C is called the **alto clef.**

Example 2.11
The Alto Clef

Although one finds the C clef placed on several other lines in older music, only the alto clef (with the clef placed on the third line) and the **tenor clef** (with the clef placed on the fourth line) are found in use today. Example 2.12 shows how the melody in Example 2.11 is notated in the tenor clef.

Example 2.12
The Tenor Clef

In a similar fashion a G clef was used centuries ago, with the G becoming stylized into what is commonly called the **treble clef:**

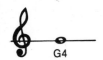

The treble clef today is placed only on the second line of the staff and identifies the G above middle C (G4). Example 2.13 shows the previous example as it is notated at the same pitch in the treble clef.

Example 2.13
The Treble Clef

The remaining clef in use today is the F clef, commonly known as the **bass clef:**

It is placed on the fourth line and identifies the F below middle C (F3). The bass clef notation for the melody we have been using as an illustration is shown in Example 2.14.

Example 2.14
The Bass Clef

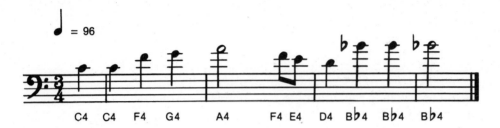

With this example, we begin to see why it is useful to have different clefs available. Notice that several ledger lines must be used to notate this example at the same pitches as those in Examples 2.10 through 2.13. And, although ledger lines are consistently employed in notation, their excessive use creates undue performance problems. To illustrate, let us take a well-known configuration as it is written for the trombone and write it three octaves higher for the flute, using the same clef!

Example 2.15
The Need for Multiple Clefs

Impractical as this is, we could theoretically write the flute part as shown if we chose to do so. Or we could write it one octave lower and place over the passage an **8va sign** (the symbol which instructs the performer to play an octave higher than written).

Example 2.16
The 8va Sign*

---

*   The *"va"* (abbreviation for "ottava," the Italian word for "at the octave") is often omitted from this octave transposition sign. Similarly, the *"ma"* (abbreviation for "quindicesima," meaning "at the fifteenth") may be omitted from the double octave transposition sign. The octave transposition sign may also be placed *below* a musical line, indicating performance at the octave below.

Or we could write it two octaves lower and place over the passage a **15ma sign** (the symbol for playing two octaves higher).

Example 2.17
The 15ma Sign*

FLUTE

But how much more efficient it is to have a special clef (the treble clef) for the flute and for other high-pitched instruments or voices.

Example 2.18
The Treble Clef

FLUTE

Since this is the case, the bass clef versions of the flute part (Examples 2.15 through 2.17) are not, in practice, acceptable. A clef appropriate to the range of each instrument exists and the appropriate clef must be used. A later discussion of instruments will specify which clefs are required for instruments in current use, and further instrumental study will indicate the extent to which octave transposition signs and ledger lines may properly be used.

Because of their extreme range, keyboard instruments use the **grand staff**, a combination of two five-line staffs. Normally, the treble clef is placed on the upper staff and the bass clef on the lower staff. Occasionally, however, the bass clef will be used in both upper and lower staffs when both hands are playing in the lower extremities of the range. Or two treble clefs will be used when both hands are playing in the upper extremities. And, although the upper staff is generally assigned to the right hand and the lower staff to the left, notes for both hands will occasionally be written on only one of the staffs.

Example 2.19
Beethoven, *Piano Sonata*, Op. 53, Movement I

Allegro con brio

The relationship between the treble and bass clefs on the grand staff can best be illustrated by moving the upper and lower staffs closer together until only one ledger line separates them, as shown in Example 2.20. The C clef is also shown in its proper relationship, but this is a redundancy supplied here only for the purpose of instruction. (The C clef is not used for keyboard music.)

Example 2.20
A Composite Staff and the Three Clefs

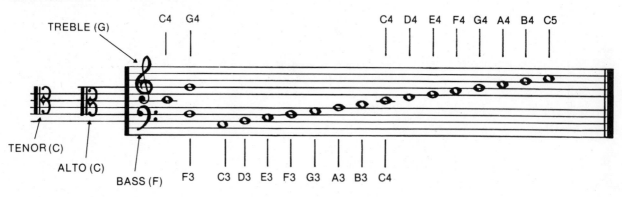

The grand staff in use today, however, separates the upper from the lower staff in order that ledger lines can be better used between staffs.

Example 2.21
The Grand Staff

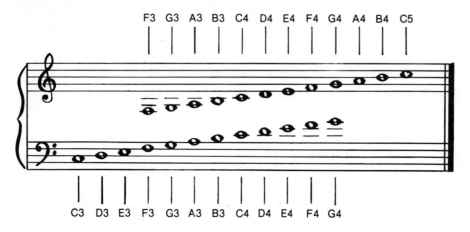

CHECK YOUR UNDERSTANDING _____

Chapter 2, No. 4

1. Draw ten or more of each clef sign, copying the model as nearly as possible.

a)

b)

c)

2. a) The first clef shown in Question 1 is called the _____ clef; also the

    _____ clef.

    b) The second clef shown is called the _____ clef; also the _____
    clef.

    c) The third clef shown is called the _____ clef; also the_____
    clef.

3. Draw several whole, half, quarter, eighth, and sixteenth notes on the staffs
    below, copying the models as nearly as possible. Notice the shading on the

    note heads ♩ and on the flags ♪ . Stems join the note heads on the left side
    and extend downward when the note head is on the middle line or above. Stems
    join the note heads on the right side and extend upward for notes below the
    middle line. Stems are usually an octave in length but they never stop short of
    the third line. (Make some use, below, of notes on or above ledger lines.)

4.   Name the pitches below. The first is solved as an example. (Octave designations are not requested.)

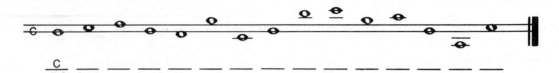

5.   Name the pitches below.

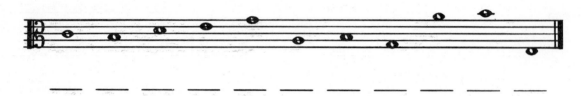

6.   Name the pitches below.

What is the name of the C clef above? _____

7.   Name the pitches below.

8.   Name the pitches below. Show the correct octave according to the system illustrated in Example 2.7. The first is solved as an example.

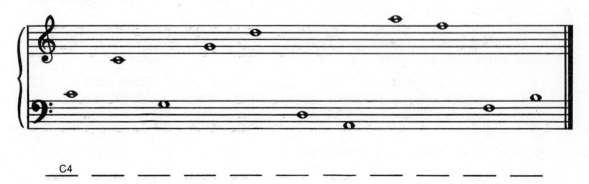

(continued)

_____
(Name)

9. Rewrite the following notes an octave lower. Make them sound the same pitches as in the model by placing the *8va* sign over the entire series. (Refer to Example 2.16.)

Model

10. Write notes of various durations on the grand staff as instructed.

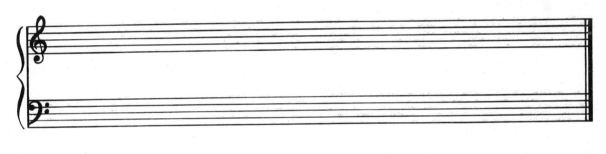

C4   C5   F♯4   A♭2   F2   B1   G3   D♭4   C♯6   D5   C7   C𝄪3

11. Write enharmonic equivalents for the given notes. The first is solved as an example.

12. Among the following, underscore only those terms or symbols that refer to the *notation of pitch*.

A4   C1   unit-pattern   G♯6   staff   pulse   grand staff
C clef   staff lines   clef signs   ascending pitches   ledger lines
timbre   tenor clef   regular division   bass clef   nonperiodic
8va   stress   15ma

(Be sure you can define all of the above.)

STAFF FOR SKETCHING

INTERVALS

General Interval Size

We have previously defined an interval as the distance between two pitches. The greater the difference between the frequencies of two pitches, the larger the interval. The interval between A = 440 and A = 880 is called a perfect octave. Example 2.22 shows several perfect octaves among the many possible.

Example 2.22
Perfect Octaves

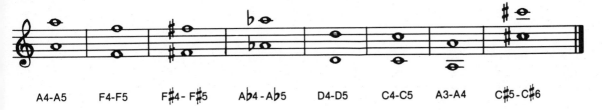

A4-A5   F4-F5   F♯4- F♯5   A♭4 -A♭5   D4-D5   C4-C5   A3-A4   C♯5-C♯6

Notice that in all octaves both pitches must have the same letter name: A3-A4, C4-C5, A♭4-A♭5, etc. When the interval A♭4-G♯5 is played, it *sounds* the same as the interval A♭4-A♭5; nevertheless, it is not *spelled* as an octave and cannot be so classified.

Interval nomenclature depends upon two factors: (1) the **general** size of the interval, as determined by spelling with alteration signs ignored, and (2) the **specific size**. The *general* interval of an octave could have any of the following spellings: C4 to C5, C4 to C♯5, C♭4 to C5. Since we are looking at the letter names of the pitches only, there is some variation in the number of steps included in the interval. By contrast the *specific* interval that is called a *perfect* octave has a fixed size of 6 whole steps: C4 to C5, C♯4 to C♯5, C♭4 to C♭5, etc.

Example 2.23 shows the calculation of several general intervals from the pitch F4. Calling F4 *one,* we can count upward (to the right) or downward (to the left) to arrive at any desired interval.

Example 2.23
The Calculation of General Intervals

PITCHES		C4	D4	E4	F4	G4	GENERAL INTERVAL
F4 up to G4	Count:				1	2	2nd
F4 down to D4	Count:		3	2	1		3rd
F4 down to E4	Count:			2	1		2nd
F4 down to C4	Count:	4	3	2	1		4th

Example 2.24 shows the staff notation of all the general intervals from the prime through the octave. Again, our illustration is based on the intervals above and below F4, but we could have started from any other point and the same principles would apply.

Example 2.24
Staff Notation of Intervals

Prime* 2nd 3rd 4th 5th 6th 7th 8ve Prime 2nd 3rd 4th 5th 6th 7th 8ve

Intervals beyond the octave (**compound intervals**) are called 9ths, 10ths, 11ths, 12ths, 13ths, 14ths, and 15ths (the double octave). Or one may refer to them as "an octave and a second," "an octave and a third," etc.

Specific Interval Size

One often needs to be more specific in interval designation. For example, F4 to A4 and F4 to Ab4 are both thirds, but the interval from F4 to Ab4 is obviously a half-step smaller than the one from F4 to A4. For a more accurate nomenclature, the general name of the interval (second, third, etc.) must be supplemented by something that accounts for the specific **quality of the interval**. Specific interval sizes are indicated by using the following adjectives: major (Maj. or M), minor (min. or m), perfect (P), diminished (dim. or d), and augmented (Aug. or A). (Doubly augmented and doubly diminished intervals are possible but their occurrence is too rare to warrant consideration at this time.)

There are certain limitations to the use of these descriptive adjectives, all dictated by historical practice.

Major and minor intervals: Only seconds, thirds, sixths, and sevenths can be major or minor.

Perfect intervals: Only primes, fourths, fifths, and octaves can be perfect.

Diminished and augmented intervals: All intervals can become diminished or augmented except the prime, which cannot be made smaller (diminished).

Specific intervals can be measured by the number of whole or half steps included. Example 2.25 illustrates this for each interval as calculated from C; however, it should be obvious that interval content holds true regardless of direction or the tone on which an interval is formed.†

---

*   **Primes** are also called **unisons**.

†   Unless you are familiar with the piano keyboard, refer to it constantly throughout this chapter. Playing and singing all examples is strongly urged.

Example 2.25
Table of Intervals

EXAMPLE	INTERVAL		STEPS
C — C	P1	(perfect prime)	0
C♯ — D♭	d2	(diminished 2nd)	0
C — C♯	A1	(augmented prime)	½
C — D♭	m2	(minor 2nd)	½
C — D	M2	(major 2nd)	1
C♯ — E♭	d3	(diminished 3rd)	1
C — D♯	A2	(augmented 2nd)	1½
C — E♭	m3	(minor 3rd)	1½
C — E	M3	(major 3rd)	2
C — F♭	d4	(diminished 4th)	2
C — E♯	A3	(augmented 3rd)	2½
C — F	P4	(perfect 4th)	2½
C — F♯*	A4	(augmented 4th)	3
C — G♭*	d5	(diminished 5th)	3
C — G	P5	(perfect fifth)	3½
C♯ — A♭	d6	(diminished 6th)	3½
C — G♯	A5	(augmented 5th)	4
C — A♭	m6	(minor 6th)	4
C — A	M6	(major 6th)	4½
C♯ — B♭	d7	(diminished 7th)	4½
C — A♯	A6	(augmented 6th)	5
C — B♭	m7	(minor 7th)	5
C — B	M7	(major 7th)	5½
C — C♭	d8	(diminished 8ve)	5½
C — B♯	A7	(augmented 7th)	6
C — C	P8	(perfect octave)	6
C — C♯	A8	(augmented 8ve)	6½

The following table diagrams the steps taken to transform given specific intervals to other specific intervals with the same general name.

Example 2.26
Transformation of Intervals

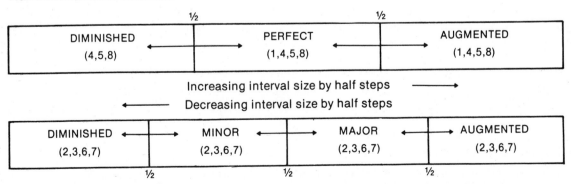

* The interval of the augmented fourth, as well as the diminished fifth, is called a **tritone** (three tones, or whole steps).

Example 2.26 shows, for example, that if an augmented prime, fourth, fifth, or octave is decreased in size by a half step (either by lowering the top note or by raising the lower) it becomes perfect. If, in turn, a perfect fourth, fifth, or octave is decreased by a half step it becomes diminished. (The perfect prime cannot be decreased in size.) On the other hand, if an augmented second, third, sixth, or seventh is decreased in size by a half step it becomes major. If decreased by another half step it becomes minor, and if decreased by still another, it becomes diminished. This assumes, of course, that the general name of the interval remains the same. For example, F♭ up to B♯ is called a fourth, even though it contains four whole steps and thus *sounds* the same as a minor sixth.

A staff example illustrating some of the intervals shown in Example 2.26 will help further in learning how specific intervals change quality.

Example 2.27
Transformation of Interval Quality (Staff)

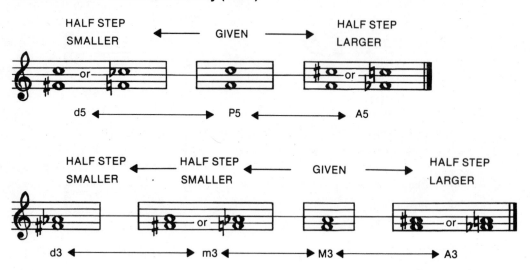

CHECK YOUR UNDERSTANDING

Chapter 2, No. 5

1. Write perfect octaves either above or below the given notes. The first is solved as an example.

2. Considering only the *general* interval size, write the designated intervals *above* the given notes. The first is solved as an example.

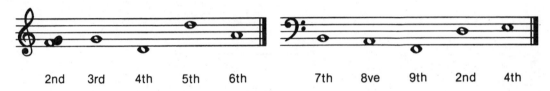

        2nd   3rd   4th   5th   6th   7th   8ve   9th   2nd   4th

3. Considering only the *general* interval size, write the designated intervals *below* the given notes. The first is solved as an example.

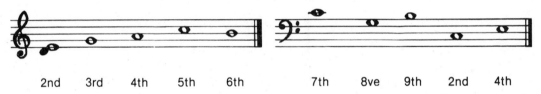

        2nd   3rd   4th   5th   6th   7th   8ve   9th   2nd   4th

4. Name all of the intervals that can be classified as

    a) perfect: _____

    b) major: _____

    c) minor: _____

    d) augmented: _____

    _____

    e) diminished: _____

    _____

5. A major interval decreased in size by a half step becomes a _____ interval.

6. A minor interval decreased in size by a half step becomes a _____ interval.

7. A perfect interval increased in size by a half step becomes an _____ interval.

8. A perfect interval decreased in size by a half step becomes a _____ interval.

9. A major third can be changed to a minor third by lowering the upper note a half step or by _____

10. Supply the number of steps (1 = whole step, ½ = half step, etc.) in the following intervals. The first is solved as an example.

Interval	Steps	Interval	Steps	Interval	Steps
a) M2	1	b) P5	_____	c) m2	_____
d) P4	_____	e) A4	_____	f) m3	_____

11. Name the following *specific* intervals. The first is solved as an example.

    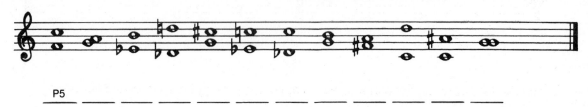

    P5 ___ ___ ___ ___ ___ ___ ___ ___ ___ ___

12. Write the designated intervals *above* the given notes. The first is solved as an example.

    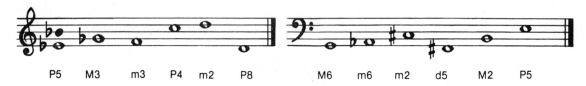

    P5   M3   m3   P4   m2   P8   M6   m6   m2   d5   M2   P5

13. Write the designated intervals *below* the given notes. The first is solved as an example.

    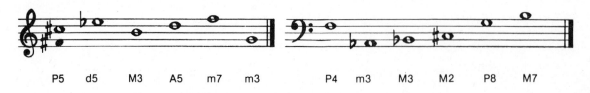

    P5   d5   M3   A5   m7   m3   P4   m3   M3   M2   P8   M7

14. Among the following, underscore only those terms or symbols that refer to *intervals*.

    general interval   perfect octave   intensity   specific interval
    timbre   primes   diminished fifth   major sixth   accent
    pace   tritone   perfect fifth   interval quality   tempo

    (Be sure you can define all of the above.)

INVERSION OF INTERVALS

The simplest kind of **interval inversion** (inversion at the octave) results from moving the lower note of a **harmonic interval** * an octave higher so that it appears above the upper note, or from moving the higher note an octave lower so that it appears below the upper note. (We are, of course, referring to **simple intervals**—those within the octave.)

Example 2.28
Inversion of General Intervals

Prime 8ve   2nd 7th   3rd 6th   4th 5th   5th 4th   6th 3rd   7th 2nd   8ve Prime

Notice that when it is inverted, a second becomes a seventh, and similarly a third becomes a sixth, etc. In each instance of inversion, the sum of the two intervals equals nine: $2 + 7 = 9$; $3 + 6 = 9$; $4 + 5 = 9$; etc. Notice also that since seconds invert to sevenths, then sevenths invert to seconds.

The principle above accounts for the effect that inversion has on the nomenclature of *general* intervals: seconds, thirds, etc.. But we also need to know how inversion affects *specific* intervals. The rules here are relatively simple:

A *major* interval inverts to a *minor* interval.

A *minor* interval inverts to a *major* interval.

A *perfect* interval inverts to a *perfect* interval.

A *diminished* interval inverts to an *augmented* interval.

An *augmented* interval inverts to a *diminished* interval.

Putting these two principles together, we find that a major third inverts to a minor sixth, a perfect fourth to a perfect fifth, a minor second to a major seventh, etc. This is a system which you will find extremely useful in the future study of music.

In spelling large intervals it may be easier at this point to think of that interval's inversion and then make the appropriate octave transposition. For example, to spell a major seventh above middle C, think as follows.

The inversion of a M 7   Raise the lower note, B3,
above C4 is a m2 below: B3.   an octave higher to B4.

m2   M7

The answer is: B4. Several staff examples are shown in Example 2.29.

---

*   A harmonic interval is one resulting from vertical alignment and simultaneous sounding of pitches. *Melodic* intervals are discussed in Chapter 3.

Example 2.29
Inversion of Specific Intervals

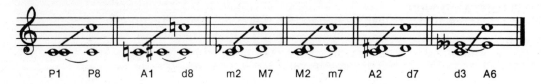

P1   P8   A1   d8   m2   M7   M2   m7   A2   d7   d3   A6

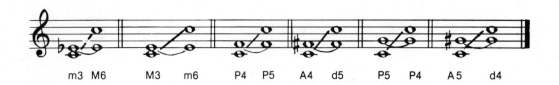

m3 M6   M3   m6   P4 P5   A4   d5   P5   P4   A5   d4

m6 M3   M6   m3   A6   d3   m7   M2   M7   m2   P8   P1

The study of scales in Chapter 3 and of triads in the next section will reinforce your present knowledge of intervals, but a word of caution is appropriate here: Your thorough understanding of more advanced harmonic principles will, to a large degree, depend upon your comprehension of the materials presented in these first two chapters. Make sure that you not only understand this material well, but can use the information without any hesitation. It has wisely been said that musicians should know the fundamentals of music as well as they know their own names!

CHECK YOUR UNDERSTANDING

Chapter 2, No. 6

1. Considering only the *general* names of the intervals, show the inversions of the following. The first is solved as an example.

Interval	Inversion	Interval	Inversion
a) prime	octave	b) 2nd	_____
c) 3rd	_____	d) 4th	_____
e) 5th	_____	f) 6th	_____
g) 7th	_____	h) octave	_____

2. Considering only the *general* names of the intervals, write the inversions of the following intervals on the staff. Analyze. The first is solved as an example.

a) Invert by moving the lower note *above* the other.

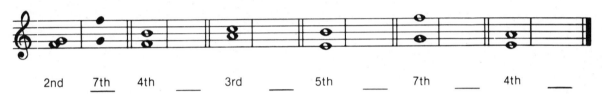

2nd   7th   4th ____   3rd ____   5th ____   7th ____   4th ____

b) Invert by moving the upper note *below* the other.

3rd   6th   6th ____   3rd ____   7th ____   6th ____   Prime ____

3. Invert the following *specific* intervals by moving the lower note above the other. Analyze. The first is solved as an example.

m3   M6   M6 ____   A5 ____   M7 ____   M3 ____   d5 ____

P4 ____   m2 ____   P5 ____   M2 ____   A2 ____   m3 ____

4.   Among the following, underscore only those terms or symbols that refer to *intervals*.

M6   P5   bar   flag   inversion   specific intervals   Hz
simple   A4   compound   harmonic interval   seventh
tenth   tritone   tie

(Be sure you can define all of the above.)

TRIADS

If all of the music written in the past 400 years were analyzed to determine the predominant chords used, *major* and *minor triads* would outnumber all others. A **chord** results when three or more tones are sounded simultaneously. In the so-called **tertian system** of harmony (and this is our primary concern in this book), chords are built by two or more superimposed intervals of thirds. A chord of three tones is called a **triad**. Example 2.30 illustrates how a triad is constructed and names its members. The clef sign has been omitted intentionally to make it clear that we are concerned with *general* rather than *specific* intervals.

Example 2.30
Constructing a Triad

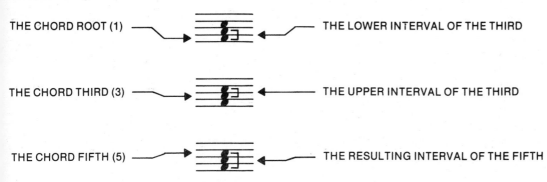

THE CHORD ROOT (1) ————————→   ←———————— THE LOWER INTERVAL OF THE THIRD

THE CHORD THIRD (3) ————————→   ←———————— THE UPPER INTERVAL OF THE THIRD

THE CHORD FIFTH (5) ————————→   ←———————— THE RESULTING INTERVAL OF THE FIFTH

For the four traditional triad types to be discussed, the thirds may be either major or minor. The interval of the fifth may be perfect, diminished, or augmented; the types of thirds that are used will determine the kinds of fifths. The four triad types are defined and illustrated in Example 2.31. Each type is built with its root on G4.

Example 2.31
Triad Types (Quality)

When the lower third is a...	and the upper third is a...	the resulting fifth is a...	and the triad is called...	Example
M3	m3	P5	major	
m3	M3	P5	minor	
m3	m3	d5	diminished	
M3	M3	A5	augmented	

M3 = major 3rd; m3 = minor 3rd; P5 = perfect 5th; d5 = diminished 5th; A5 = augmented 5th.

The major triad is so named because the lower interval of the third is a major third; the minor triad, because the lower third is minor; the diminished triad, because the resulting fifth is a diminished fifth; and the augmented triad, because the resulting fifth is augmented.

Triads are identified according to both the *quality* of the triad (the precise type: major, minor, diminished, or augmented) and the *name* of the specific triad (the note on which the triad is built, the root). The following symbols will be used.*

Example 2.32
Triad Nomenclature

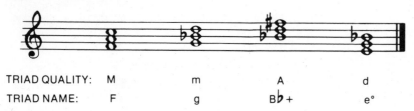

TRIAD QUALITY:	M	m	A	d
TRIAD NAME:	F	g	B♭+	e°

Notice that for the *major* triad an upper case letter is used in analysis to indicate both triad quality and name. For the *minor* triad a lower case letter is used for both. For the *augmented* triad an upper case letter is used to designate quality, but in naming the triad a "plus" (+) is added. For the *diminished* triad a lower case letter is used, but in naming the triad a small circle (°) is added. (Refer again to Example 2.32.)

The consecutive order of the alphabet to name scales

A B C D E F G A
1 2 3 4 5 6 7 8

is known as the **basic scale**. To construct the basic chord alphabet, we derive a new series from the scale alphabet by **permutation**, that is, by varying the order as follows: 1, 3, 5, 7, 2, 4, 6, 8, which arranges the series in thirds:

A C E G B D F A
1 3 5 7 2 4 6 8

From this chord alphabet we can derive the seven **basic triads** formed on the white keys. Three of the triads are major, three are minor, and one is diminished.

Example 2.33
The Seven Basic Triads

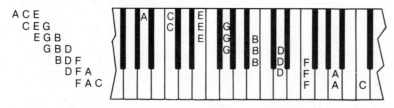

MAJOR		MINOR		DIMINISHED
F A C G B D		D F A E G B		B D F
C E G		A C E		

---

*   Also refer to Appendix 2.

The ability to spell quickly all kinds of triads, using any given note as the root, third, or fifth, is essential to anyone planning to continue music study. Spelling facility can be achieved by several approaches. To start with, you can simply practice identifying the intervals between tones of a given triad. For example, a B♭ major triad has a tone (D) a major third above the root and a tone (F) a minor third above D (or a perfect fifth above the root).

Another approach to the problem is to use symbolic representations. These can help you to visualize the differences among the four triad types and can be useful when changing from one type to another. In the following diagram, each bar (or finger) represents triad member 1,3, or 5. Learn the symbols for each type.

Example 2.34
Diagrammatic Symbols for Triads

TRIAD TYPE	DIAGRAMMATIC SYMBOL	HAND DIAGRAMS
Augmented	5 / 3 / 1	
Major	5 / 3 / 1	
Minor	5 / 3 / 1	
Diminished	5 / 3 / 1	

A wide space represents the interval of the major third, a narrow one that of the minor third. But bear in mind that triads must always maintain their spelling in thirds: C E G, C E♭ G, C E♭ G♭, etc.—never C D♯ G, even though enharmonically the sound is the same as C E♭ G. Example 2.35 illustrates how the above symbols can be used in changing triad types.

Example 2.35
Triad Transformation

To change the following triad...	whose symbol is...	to this triad...	whose symbol is...	the solution is..
C	▬▬ G ▬▬ E ▬▬ C	c	▬▬ ▬▬ ▬▬	Lower the third C E♭ G
C	▬▬ G ▬▬ E ▬▬ C	c♯	▬▬ ▬▬ ▬▬	Raise the root and fifth C♯ E G♯
a♭	▬▬ E♭ ▬▬ c♭ ▬▬ A♭	A♭+	▬▬ ▬▬ ▬▬	Raise the third and fifth A♭ C E
G+	▬▬ D♯ ▬▬ B ▬▬ G	g	▬▬ ▬▬ ▬▬	Lower the third and fifth G B♭ D

The symbols will no doubt suggest several study-games that will facilitate the spelling of triads. For "bars" (▬▬▬), erasers, chalk, or blocks of wood can be used and moved at will in drilling on triad transformation.

Perhaps the best way to spell triads comes from the sight-sound relationship resulting from aural and keyboard drill and from performing music. Eventually musicians learn to "see with their ears and hear with their eyes." When students reach this point in their mastery of music, they hear the sound of a chord (or a melody) and immediately "visualize" the notes that represent the sounds.

A triad may be heard vertically (as a simultaneous sound) or **arpeggiated** (as successively sounded chord tones):

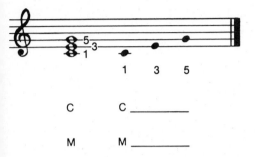

Since music is an aural art, you are urged to drill diligently on the aural identification of triads and intervals. Refer to the ADML section at the end of this chapter for suggested activities. Triad inversion, member distribution, and chord progression are presented in Chapter 2, Book II.

STAFF FOR SKETCHING

CHECK YOUR UNDERSTANDING

Chapter 2, No. 7

1. Of all the music written in recent centuries, which two chords would predominate in frequency? _____ _____ and _____ _____

2. Define a triad in your own words.

    _____

    _____

3. *In the major triad:*

    a) the interval from 1 to 3 is a _____ _____,

    b) the interval from 3 to 5 is a _____ _____,

    c) the interval from 1 to 5 is a _____ _____.

4. *In the minor triad:*

    a) the interval from 1 to 3 is a _____ _____,

    b) the interval from 3 to 5 is a _____ _____,

    c) the interval from 1 to 5 is a _____ _____.

5. *In the diminished triad:*

    a) the interval from 1 to 3 is a _____ _____,

    b) the interval from 3 to 5 is a _____ _____,

    c) the interval from 1 to 5 is a _____ _____.

6. *In the augmented triad:*

    a) the interval from 1 to 3 is a _____ _____,

    b) the interval from 3 to 5 is a _____ _____,

    c) the interval from 1 to 5 is a _____ _____.

7. Triads are constructed by the vertical stacking of intervals of the _____.

8. The note that determines the name for a triad (for example, C-major, G-major, etc.) is called the _____ of the triad.

9. Using bar symbols, draw the symbolic representation of the four triad types in the boxes at the top of the next page.

Major	Minor	Diminished	Augmented

10. Spell *major* triads by supplying the missing members of the triad. Do not change any of the given letters! The first is solved as an example.

     __A_ _C♯_ _E__   D F♯ ____   G ____ ____   E♭ ____ ____   D♭ F ____

     ____ F𝄪 ____   ____ B♭ ____   B♭ ____ ____   ____ D♯ ____   ____ ____ G

11. Spell *minor* triads by supplying missing members of the triad.

     A ____ E   ____ D ____   ____ ____ F   E♭ ____ ____   ____ E♭ ____

     D♭ ____ ____   ____ ____ B♭   D ____ ____   ____ ____ F♯   D♯ ____ ____

12. Spell *diminished* triads by supplying missing members of the triad.

     C ____ ____   D ____ ____   ____ E ____   E♭ ____ ____   ____ ____ B♭

     ____ ____ B   ____ G B♭   F♯ ____ ____   G♯ ____ ____   A ____ ____

13. Spell *augmented* triads by supplying missing members of the triad.

     C ____ ____   ____ F ____   ____ ____ A♯   ____ F♯ ____   E♭ ____ ____

     ____ A ____   G♭ ____ ____   ____ B ____   A♭ ____ ____   ____ C♯ ____

14. Using the labellings supplied in Example 2.32, identify the given triads. The first is solved as an example.

QUALITY: A __ __ __ __ __ __ __ __ __ __ __

NAME: F+ __ __ __ __ __ __ __ __ __ __ __

(continued)

QUALITY: __ __ __ __ __ __ __ __ __ __

NAME: __ __ __ __ __ __ __ __ __ __

15. Write triads on the staff as instructed. The first is solved as an example.

QUALITY:	M	M	m	m	M	d	A	M	M	m	m	d
NAME:	E♭	F	f	d	E	f♯°	G+	F♯	A♭	e	b	c♯°

QUALITY:	M	M	m	m	M	d	A	M	M	m	m	d
NAME:	G	G♭	a♯	f♯	D♭	f°	E+	C♭	B	g♯	g	f♯°

16. Among the following, underscore only those terms or symbols that refer to *tertian chords*.

pulse   meter   seventh chord   irregular division   triad
rhythm-pattern   basic triad   root   tone cluster   chord third
motion   unit-pattern   unit   chord fifth   diminished triad
measure bar   flag   tempo   major triad   e°   beat
accent   minor chord   augmented triad   G +   chord quality
measure signature

(Be sure you can define all of the above.)

STAFF FOR SKETCHING

Activities for Developing Music Literacy

AURAL AND KEYBOARD DRILL

1. Play single tones* within your vocal range on the piano (or some other instrument) and match these tones at the unison by singing on some neutral syllable such as "lah."

2. Play single tones outside your vocal range. Match these tones at the octave (or double octave, etc.).

3. Sing any tone. Sing a second tone an octave above or below.

4. Play various tones within your vocal range on the white and black keys of the piano. Match these tones at the unison by singing, using a correct name for each pitch according to the nomenclature shown in Example 2.7: C4, A3, B♭4 (or A♯4), A2, etc.

5. Play various tones outside your vocal range. Quickly name each tone played. Sing at the octave in your range. Also name the enharmonic equivalent for tones played on the black keys.

6. Write various notes on the five-line staff. Use all of the four clefs (treble, bass, alto, and tenor). Make some use of ledger lines. First, play each tone. Second, sing with correct pitch names.

Model

| F4 | B♭4 | A4 | B3 | F♯5 | D5 | C5 |

7. Follow the instructions in Drill 6 above, but write notes on the grand staff. When pitches are outside your vocal range, sing octave equivalents.

8. Listen to the playing of harmonic intervals presented in the order below. Learn to identify them aurally. Continue this drill until you become familiar with each interval.

---

*   If we wish to be absolutely explicit, we must use the word *note* to denote the symbol and the word *tone* to denote the sound. But a strict observance of this differentiation can sometimes lead to some rather awkward rhetoric. Therefore, we will often use the word *tone* to signify either the symbol or the sound. You are urged to "auralize" written notation and to think of *notes* as *tones*—as conceptualized sound.

Models

Instructor plays perfect octaves:

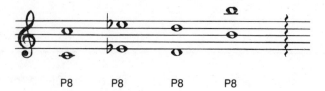

P8   P8   P8   P8

Student hears and identifies all intervals as perfect octaves.

Instructor plays perfect fifths:

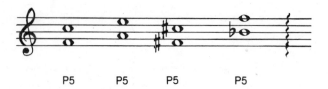

P5   P5   P5   P5

Student hears and identifies all intervals as perfect fifths.

> Continue in a similar manner for the perfect fourth, major third, minor third, major sixth, major second, minor second, major seventh, minor seventh, and the tritone (heard as either a diminished fifth or an augmented fourth).
>
> At first, you may encounter some difficulty in differentiating between the perfect fifth and perfect fourth, between the major third and the minor third, or between the major sixth and the minor sixth. Identification, however slow, will come with practice and further study.

9. The instructor plays a series of perfect octaves, inserting in the series one interval that is not a perfect octave. Identify the one interval that is different. Proceed through a series of the other intervals in a similar manner. (The one different interval can be easily identified if, for example, a minor second is inserted in a series of perfect octaves. Or it can be difficult to identify if, for example, a perfect fourth is inserted in a series of perfect fifths. Proceed slowly and cautiously!)

10. Aurally identify various kinds of intervals (general classification) played by your instructor or partner. Learn to identify a series of (a) octaves, (b) fifths, (c) seconds, (d) thirds, etc. on the white keys.

Model

Instructor plays:

Student responds: OCTAVES   FIFTHS   SECONDS   THIRDS

> Follow the above drill with one where general intervals are mixed.

Model

Instructor plays:

Student responds: 5th   4th   3rd   3rd   6th   6th   7th   7th   8ve

(Go to Drill 11 only after a reasonable degree of mastery is achieved in identifying *general* intervals.)

11. Aurally identify various kinds of intervals (specific classification) played by
your instructor or partner.

Model

Instructor plays:

Student responds: P5   P4   M3   m2   P8   m7   M7   P5   m3

12. Play various kinds of intervals on the keyboard.* Name the interval. Invert this
interval by moving the lower note an octave above. Name the interval. Return to
playing the first interval. Invert by moving the higher note an octave lower.
Name the interval. Sing each interval as follows.

Model

MAJOR 3rd   MINOR 6th   MAJOR 3rd   MINOR 6th

13. Learn to identify major triads by singing them arpeggiated upwards from the
root and back. Practice with both numbers and note names from any tone. This
aural drill will help not only in the identification of triads but also in the identification of intervals.

Model

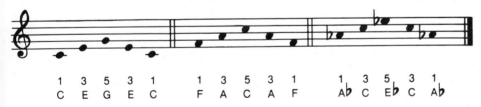

1   3   5   3   1   1   3   5   3   1   1   3   5   3   1
C   E   G   E   C   F   A   C   A   F   Ab C   Eb C   Ab

14. Sing major triads from the third as follows.

Model

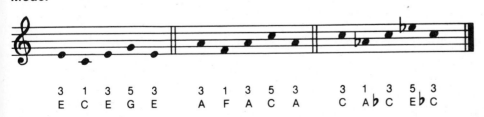

3   1   3   5   3   3   1   3   5   3   3   1   3   5   3
E   C   E   G   E   A   F   A   C   A   C   Ab C   Eb C

----

*   If a piano is not available for drill, use any keyboard instrument such as the organ,
electric piano, vibraphone, xylophone, marimba, orchestra bells, etc. (See Chapter 5 in the
next book of the series for the transpositions of the xylophone and orchestra bells.)

15.   Sing major triads from the fifth as follows.

Model

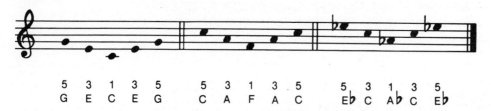

5	3	1	3	5		5	3	1	3	5		5	3	1	3	5
G	E	C	E	G		C	A	F	A	C		E♭	C	A♭	C	E♭

Practice Drills 13-15 until these three short melodic configurations are thoroughly familiar and can readily be identified by ear as a major triad. Drill 16 will demonstrate how this skill is used.

16.   Given the top voice, listen to major triads played on a keyboard instrument (or sung in three or four parts).

a) Identify the quality: M in the model below.
b) Identify the upper voice: the root (1) in the model below.
c) Identify the lower voice: the third (3) in the model below.

Once you can match the pitch of the outer voices, you should apply the information and skill gained from Drills 13–15, bringing the tones within your vocal range.

Model

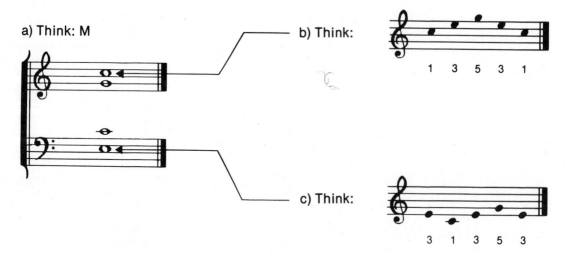

a) Think: M

b) Think:

    1   3   5   3   1

c) Think:

    3   1   3   5   3

Your response would be: M or, more precisely, C if either one of the outer voices is supplied.

(Above "M": 1 over 3; above "C": 1 over 3)

It would be incorrect to hear the upper voice configuration in the model above as the following.

    5   3   1   3   5   3   1   3   5   3

These two configurations are not melodically correct for singing from 5 or 3. C is 1, the root! This is an error you can avoid by learning the three *correct* configurations thoroughly (Drills 13–15). The first five tones of "The Star Spangled Banner" parallel the 5-3-1-3-5 configuration. Perhaps you can find tunes that parallel the other two major-chord configurations. Once you can identify the outer parts correctly as 1,3,5, there only remains the problem of determining the chord member distribution and the doubling. This study will be presented in Book II.

17.   Sing and learn to identify minor triads according to Drills 13–15.

18.   Drill on diminished and augmented triads in a similar manner.

Note: Because of the considerably less frequent use of diminished and augmented triads in music, early drill should focus on the major and minor triads. *Triad drill should follow these priorities:*

a) Learn to identify aurally the type of triad.
b) Learn to identify aurally the triad member in the outer voices.

These objectives can be best accomplished by having the instructor or another student play various triads for identification and notation on the staff.

19.   Play all four types of triads on a keyboard instrument in three parts with the right hand. Play these on any given tone with the root, third, or fifth in the lowest part.

20.   Repeat Drill 19, using the left hand.

ANALYTICAL LISTENING

1.   "Rex Domine," *Masterpieces of Music Before 1750.* Haydn Society Records HSE 9038.

This is an example of organum from around the 9th century. In this two-part vocal composition, what harmonic intervals predominate? [Refer also to *Masterpieces of Music Before 1750,* compiled and edited by Carl Parish and John F. Ohl (New York: W. W. Norton & Co., 1951) p 17.] Listen to other early music in this collection. Try to determine how you would notate the rhythm. Conduct downbeats to coincide with the pulse.

2.   Reed, *La Fiesta Mexicana.* Performed by the Eastman Wind Ensemble conducted by Frederick Fennel, Mercury Classics MG 40011; or the Eastman Wind Ensemble conducted by Donald Hunsburger, *Fiesta,* Decca Records DL 710157; or the University of Illinois Concert Band conducted by Harry Begian, University of Illinois, Record No. 36; or the Michigan State University Symphonic Band conducted by Kenneth C. Bloomquist, Audio Tape Production, MI 48876.

At the beginning of the first movement and again at the beginning of the second movement, what is the interval played by the chimes?

3.   Harris, *Symphony No. 3*. Performed by the Eastman-Rochester Orchestra conducted by Howard Hanson, Mercury Records MG 40004; or the Boston Symphony Orchestra conducted by Serge Koussevitzky, Victor Records LCT 1153.

Listen to the beginning of this symphony, which starts with unison cellos and develops chant-like until the entry of the violas creates a simple harmony of intervals of the perfect fourth.

4. Reed, "El Muchacho," *Sona Libre.* Performed by the Cal Tjader group (Clare Fischer, pianist), Verve Records V-8531.

   Listen to the long series of consecutive thirds (both major and minor thirds). Later, the thirds are inverted to sixths. The use of the interval of the third or the sixth is typical of much of the pop and folk music of Latin America.

5. Debussy *Nocturnes,* "Nuages." Performed by the Orchestre de la Suisse Romande conducted by Ernest Ansermet, London Records CS6023; or the Boston Symphony Orchestra conducted by Charles Munch, Victor Records LSC 2668.

   Listen to the long series of consecutive thirds, both major and minor. See if you can notate these thirds.

6. Copland, *The Red Pony,* Movement IIIb, Theme 2. Performed by the St. Louis Symphony conducted by André Previn, Columbia Records ML 5983.

   Although the melody is written as grace notes, the effect is one of consecutive seconds.

7. Locate passages from other compositions that feature consecutive harmonic intervals: seconds, thirds, fourths, fifths, sixths, sevenths. What is the effect achieved by consecutive intervals? Compare the movement of consecutive intervals to notes that move in contrary direction.

8. Wagner, *Das Rheingold,* "Prelude." Performed by the Vienna Philharmonic conducted by Georg Solti, London Records 1309.

   This prelude is unique in its almost exclusive use of the three tones of a major triad, E♭, G, B♭. Notice that a definite mood can be established and interest maintained with these limited harmonic and melodic resources if one has the skill to properly control the other three parameters of rhythm, form, and color. Only a very few nonchord tones appear near the end of this prelude. (Refer again to Example 1.3 or, preferably, to the complete piano reduction or full **score** of this prelude.)

9. Many rock tunes of the 60's and 70's are based on a single chord, usually a major or minor triad. Unlike the Wagner prelude, these triad tones are supplemented with nonchord tones (discussed in detail in Book II), but the basic harmonic and melodic structure is 1, 3, 5 of the triad. A few of the many are listed below.

   LaPread and Richie, "Fancy Dancers," *Hot on the Track.* Performed by the Commodores, Motown Records M6-86751.

   Klemmer, "Barefoot Ballet," *Barefoot Ballet.* Performed by John Klemmer, ABC Records A8 CP-950.

   Jagger and Richards, "Midnight Rambler," *Let It Bleed.* Performed by The Rolling Stones, London Records, NPS4. (This is a blues-rock tune based on the C-major triad. Other than a few nonchord tones, one distinctive feature is the use of E♭'s in the melody over the C-major triad. This simultaneous use of both the major and minor third is referred to as the "**split third**." The minor third is almost always found in the melody.

   Whitfield, "You've Got To Believe," *The Best of The Pointer Sisters.* Performed by the Pointer Sisters, ABC Records BTSY-6026/2

   James, "Storm King," *Bob James 3.* Performed by Bob James with Grover Washington on the alto Saxophone, CTI Records CTI 6063.

IMPROVISATION

1. At your own tempo, using pulses, divisions, ties between pulses, and rests, experiment with the sounds of specific harmonic intervals. Use a keyboard instrument. Try to create fascinating music.

   a) Use only perfect fifths.

Model

Soft and connected   ♩ = 60

   b) Proceed as above, but use major and minor thirds.
   c) Use major and minor sixths.
   d) Use only major sevenths. Explore the entire range of the piano and its dynamic levels. Experiment with the pedals to learn how they function.
   e) Proceed as in part (d) above, but use a variety of intervals.

2. Improvise with two students at the keyboard and a third acting as conductor. Choose one interval (perfect fifth, for example) to be played in tempo by both performers. Although both will be playing perfect fifths, chance will preclude the same fifths from falling together often.

Model

Soft and connected   ♩ = 60

3. Proceed as in Improvisation 2, but experiment with intervals other than the perfect fifth.

4. Proceed as above, but experiment with the use of a different interval for each performer. For example, one player uses thirds (major and minor) while the other player uses perfect fifths.

5. If your keyboard technique is adequate, improvise as above using both hands. (These improvisations should never "plod along" but should be as sensitive and as musical as possible, using the material presented to date.)

Note: Mallet percussion instruments may be used if other keyboard instruments are not available.

6.   Improvise a melody using only the root, third, and fifth of a major or a minor triad. Since the harmonic parameter (H) will not exist and the melodic parameter (M) will be greatly depressed due to limiting melodic movement to the root, third, and fifth of a triad, great skill must be exerted to elevate the other three parameters (R, F, and C). Of course, the form and color parameters can be controlled better after their study in Chapters 4 and 5.

7.   Follow the instructions in Exercise 6, but add one or more instruments. Again, limit the tones used to the root, third, and fifth of a single triad. With three or more voices, the result should be a simple kind of **polyphonic** music. The goal is to create as interesting a piece as possible with the limited melodic means. Best results will come from choosing instruments or voices in contrasting ranges. A conductor may be used to help maintain a steady, predetermined tempo; or you may wish to explore a free rhythm with no uniform pulse. Percussion instruments may be used.

CREATIVE WRITING

1.   Write a short composition for piano, or for two voices, or two instruments. Use only perfect fifths. Use only pulses, divisions, ties between pulses, and rests. Choose your tempo and dynamic levels. Refer to the model in Improvisation 1(a) for a suggestion on how to prepare your score. Bring your composition to a convincing close. Perform, record, and replay for class evaluation.

2.   Write a short composition following the instructions above, but choose a single interval other than the perfect fifth. The interval can move quite widely in range if written for instruments (so long as the parts remain within the range of the instrument being used); but if for voices, the range should be considerably less extensive.

3.   Write a short composition similar to Improvisation 2, 3, or 4. If for other than piano, choose instruments or voices to match the ranges you plan to use.

4.   Write a short composition similar to Improvisation 6 for a solo instrument or voice.

5.   Write a short composition similar to Improvisation 7 for three instruments or voices. Prepare a neat and accurate score (with a separate part for each performer) and perform in class.

Note: Choosing pitches, note values, tempos, etc., should be governed by your aesthetic judgment and motivated by your improvisational experience. Further study will uncover many other factors that will influence your creative decisions and enhance your music.

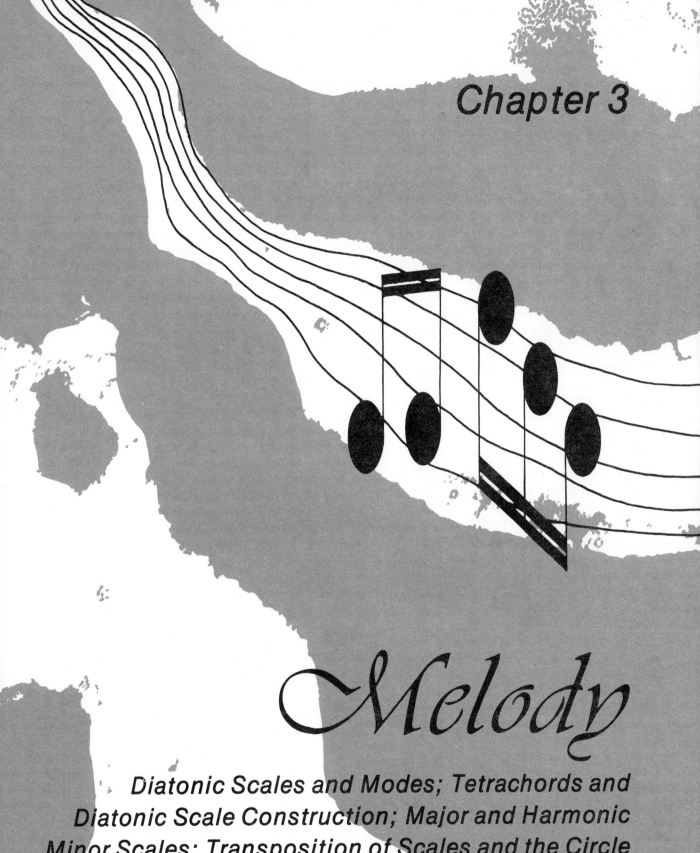

Chapter 3

Melody

Diatonic Scales and Modes; Tetrachords and
Diatonic Scale Construction; Major and Harmonic
Minor Scales; Transposition of Scales and the Circle
of Fifths; Key Signatures; Modal Key Signatures

The melodic parameter of music is closely related to the other parameters. Its interaction with rhythm and harmony is particularly strong. One cannot have pitch without duration, and a melody line usually implies a harmony. The ways in which the five basic parameters of music interact will be discussed in more detail in Book II, and this study will further reinforce your understanding of melody.

A **melody** can be thought of as an orderly, horizontal succession of tones heard as the dominating line. Although often regarded as a scalewise and chordal line, melody may also be an orderly arrangement of widely separated tones from the twelve tones in our tempered scale, an arrangement of various tones in the quarter-tone or other tuning system, or electronic or computer-generated lines. This chapter, however, presents only **diatonic scales** and **modes,** the building material of diatonic melodies. To understand melody is to understand scales.

DIATONIC SCALES AND MODES

A **diatonic scale** is a succession of eight different tones within the octave, each tone being separated from the other by either a half or a whole step. The first tone of the scale (the **tonic**) complements the scale by being repeated as the eighth tone an octave higher thereby making the scale a combination of two intervals of the fourth,

$$\overbrace{\text{A, B, C, D,}}^{\text{4th}} \qquad \overbrace{\text{E, F, G, A,}}^{\text{4th}}$$

for example. All seven* letters (A,B,C,D,E,F,G) must be present and must together produce some combination of five whole steps and two half steps. To be diatonic, each half of the scale (tones 1 through 4 and 5 through 8)† must contain no more than one minor second. Nor can half steps occur in consecutive order, otherwise the scale takes on a chromatic quality.

Seven of the most common diatonic scales, commonly called **modes**, can be heard by playing on the white keys of the piano.

Example 3.1
The Seven Diatonic Modes Available on the White Keys

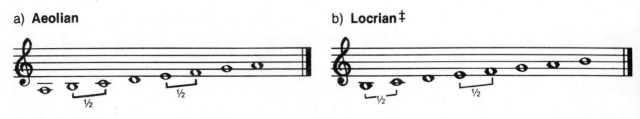

a) **Aeolian**   b) **Locrian** ‡

---

*   Further study of theory and music literature will show that there are many other scale types: scales with five tones within the octave (**pentatonic scales**), scales with six tones within the octave (**whole-tone scales**, for example), and scales of more than seven different tones. Chapter 2 introduced the chromatic scale, which has twelve tones within the octave.

†   Refer to the next section, "Tetrachords and Diatonic Scale Construction," for further clarification.

‡   The Locrian mode was not used to any great extent in any period, probably because its scale members 1,3,5 form a diminished triad, a chord which lacks the finality of the major and minor tonic triads of the other modes. It will hereafter receive but little attention.

c) **Ionian**   d) **Dorian**

e) **Phrygian**   f) **Lydian**

g) **Mixolydian**

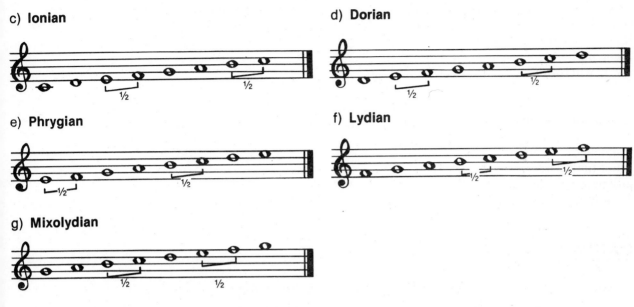

The names given in Example 3.1 are those used to identify the church modes of the Medieval and Renaissance periods. These modes are further identified according to their first and last tones. Diatonic scales (to include the modes) are numbered from the first tone (the tonic) upward: 1, 2, 3, 4, 5, 6, 7, 8. The modes in Example 3.1 would be called A Aeolian (or Aeolian on A), B Locrian (or Locrian on B), C Ionian, D Dorian, E Phrygian, F Lydian, and G Mixolydian. This distinction is required since it is possible to **transpose** and write scales starting on any one of the twelve pitches.

There is a slight difference between a "mode" and a "scale," but the difference is primarily of historical interest.* When using the names given in Example 3.1, we will refer to these constructions as modes. The term "scale" has a more general meaning, encompassing all kinds of formations. (See the footnote at the beginning of this section.) But the word "scale" is also used in a more specific way, for example, when we speak of a **major scale** or a **minor scale.**

To avoid a common misconception, one should remember that music came before the scale, although a composer generally has a scale structure or some pitch collection in mind before starting to compose. Written scales are only diagrammatical representations of the musical content; but, as every instrumental and vocal student knows, they are also used to develop playing technique—probably because so many melodies are based on scalewise movement. The first four measures of an old fiddle tune, "Give the Fiddler a Dram," illustrate this point.

Example 3.2
"Give the Fiddler a Dram" (Folk)†

---

* There is also a difference in the way harmony is handled. This aspect of modality will be discussed in a later book.

† The symbol ➤ is a **dynamic accent** signifying greater intensity. The curved line is a **slur** indicating performance without break between pitches.

Deriving the correct scale from this **diatonic melody** is a technique more under-standable after the study of **tonality**, but here we base our conclusion on two clues: (1) The final tone is C, and the final tone is usually the focal tone, or **tonic**, after which the scale is named. (2) C, E, and G are important **structural tones,** and these form a tonic triad on C.

The scale derived from "Give the Fiddler a Dram" is shown in Example 3.3. We say that the tune is **in the key** of C, or has the **tonality** of C, and we refer to C as the **tonic center** or **key center.**

Example 3.3
Derived Scale

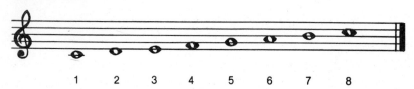

Each of the scale members has a name. The scale shown in Example 3.3, which you may have recognized as the C-Ionian mode, will serve as an illustration. In Example 3.4, after examining part (a), study the rearrangement of the scale in part (b) as an aid to remembering the names.

Example 3.4
Names for the Scale Members

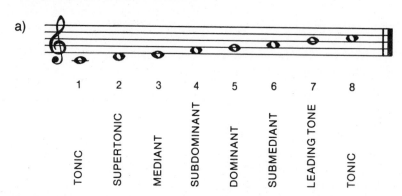

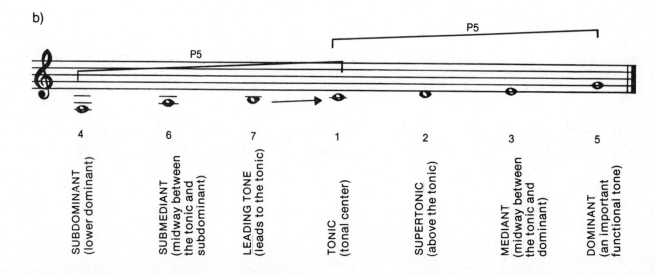

The same terminology is used for the scale members in all of the modes. An exception to the above nomenclature occurs when the seventh scale member is a major second* below the tonic (rather than a minor second). In this case the seventh member is called the **subtonic** rather than the **leading tone.** Later study of harmony will show that these same names are used for the chords built on these scale members.

---

*   Harmonic intervals were explained in detail in Chapter 2. The nomenclature for intervals remains the same when measuring the distance between tones in a scale or melody, but since the pitches are heard successively rather than simultaneously, we refer to the intervals as **melodic intervals**.

STAFF FOR SKETCHING

CHECK YOUR UNDERSTANDING

Chapter 3, No. 1

1. Define *melody* in your own words. _____

   _____

   _____

2. A diatonic scale is a succession of _____ different tones within the
   octave with each tone separated from the other by either a _____ or
   _____ step. The first tone of the scale (the _____) complements the scale by being repeated as the _____ tone an octave
   higher. All seven letters (_____ _____ _____ _____ _____ _____ _____)
   must produce some combination of _____ whole steps and _____
   half steps. The _____ _____ should not occur in consecutive order.

3. The first tone of a diatonic scale is called the _____

4. There are _____ basic diatonic scales available on the white keys.

5. Name the seven church modes built on the white keys and starting on the given
   tonics.

   a) On A: _____   b) On B: _____

   c) On C: _____   d) On D: _____

   e) On E: _____   f) On F: _____

   g) On G: _____

6. Supply the letter name for the designated member of each mode as instructed.
   The first is solved as an example.

Member	Scale	Letter Name	Member	Scale	Letter Name
a) 4	Mixolydian on G	____	b) 1	Ionian on C	____
c) 5	Phrygian on E	____	d) 3	Dorian on D	____
e) 2	Lydian on F	____	f) 3	Aeolian on A	____

7. The last eight measures of the early American folk song "Home on the Range" are shown below. This tune is constructed on one of the seven basic scales. Derive the scale and write it on the staff supplied. Name the scale.

Derived scale: _____

Scale name: _____

8. Write the melody of some diatonic melody you know or have performed. Derive the scale as above. (A melody without alteration signs will be easier for the beginner.)

Derived scale: _____

Scale name: _____

9. Supply the correct technical names for the following scale members. The first is solved as an example.

    a) Scale member 1: _____tonic_____

    b) Scale member 2: _____

    c) Scale member 3: _____

    d) Scale member 4: _____

    e) Scale member 5: _____

    f) Scale member 6: _____

    g) Scale member 7 _____ or _____

    h) Scale member 8: _____

(continued)

10. Name the following melodic intervals. The first is solved as an example.

a)

b)

c)

d)

11. Among the following, underscore only those terms or symbols that refer to _scales or modes._

   diatonic   beat   measure   chromatic   beam   tonic
   M6   P4   Aeolian   whole-tone scale   Ionian mode   Phrygian
   octave   _8va_   mode   frequency   dominant   subtonic
   ledger lines   regular division   leading tone   derived scale

   (Be sure you can define all of the above.)

STAFF FOR SKETCHING

TETRACHORDS AND DIATONIC SCALE CONSTRUCTION

Before proceeding further, we need to understand another term: **tetrachord**, coming from the Greek *tetrachordos*, meaning four-stringed. The word tetrachord today refers to four consecutive tones: A, B, C, D; B, C, D, E; C, D, E, F; etc. Our discussion of diatonic scale construction will begin with a look at those tetrachords derived from the white keys of the piano keyboard and how they are used as building blocks in forming diatonic scales. Each diatonic scale (or mode) will have a lower tetrachord of four notes and an upper tetrachord of four notes, counting the repetition of the tonic. Notice in Example 3.5 that four possible types of tetrachords are realized from the white keys. Each differs in its arrangement of the whole and half steps.

Example 3.5
Tetrachords

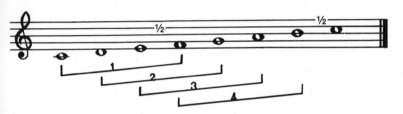

The chart below shows (a) the tetrachord type number, (b) the tetrachord spelling in letter names, (c) the interval between scale members (M = major second, m = minor second), (d) the number of steps between scale members (1 = whole step, ½ = half step) and (e) the diagrammatic pattern, in which the larger distance between circles equals whole steps and the smaller distance equals half steps.

TYPE	TETRACHORD	INTERVAL	STEP	DIAGRAMMATIC PATTERN*
1	C D E F	M M m	1 1 ½	● ● ●●
2	D E F G	M m M	1 ½ 1	● ●● ●
3	E F G A	m M M	½ 1 1	●● ● ●
4	F G A B	M M M	1 1 1	● ● ● ●

(Tetrachords starting on the next three keys merely repeat Types 1, 2, 3 above.)

1	G A B C	M M m	1 1 ½	● ● ●●
2	A B C D	M m M	1 ½ 1	● ●● ●
3	B C D E	m M M	½ 1 1	●● ● ●

* The four types of tetrachords are often named for their corresponding modes: Type 1 Ionian tetrachord; Type 2, Dorian tetrachord; Type 3, Phrygian tetrachord, and Type 4, Lydian tetrachord. Type 1,

Two consecutive tetrachords combine to form several types of seven-tone scales (eight tones, counting the repetition of the first tone.) The two consecutive tetrachords must be connected by no more than a step; otherwise the series will exceed an octave. Even so, some combinations of tetrachords exceed an octave and thus are not usable as diatonic scales. For example, the following tetrachords, though joined by only a half step, exceed the octave.

Example 3.6
A Tetrachord Combination That Fails to Form a Diatonic Scale

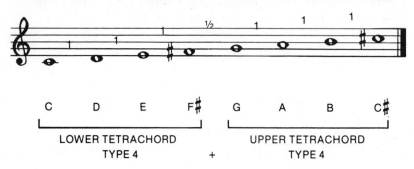

Notice that to write a Type 4 tetrachord on C, it is necessary to use alteration signs. (Alteration signs are generally required when constructing a variety of scales on a common tonic tone.)

A Type 4 tetrachord, then, must be used only with one of the other three types, and with the tetrachords joined by a half step. In the same manner, Types 1, 2, and 3 can be combined with themselves only if they are connected by a whole step; otherwise the scale will fall short of the octave by a half step.

Although some arrangements will not function as diatonic scales, it is interesting to see the results of combining each tetrachord with itself and the three other types: 1 + 1, 1 + 2, 1 + 3, and 1 + 4; 2 + 1, 2 + 2, 2 + 3, and 2 + 4; etc. Example 3.7 shows all combinations of tetrachords joined by a step (a major second). Each scale is built with C as the tonic. Those that conform to the patterns of the modes (Example 3.1) are identified by their modal names.

Example 3.7
Tetrachords Joined by a Whole Step

TYPE	SPELLING	SCALE NAME	DIAGRAMMATIC PATTERN
1 + 1	C D E F G A B C	Ionian (Major)	● ● ●● ● ● ●●
1 + 2	C D E F G A B♭ C	Mixolydian	● ● ●● ● ●● ●
1 + 3	C D E F G A♭ B♭ C	No name	● ● ●● ●● ● ●
1 + 4	C D E F G A B C♯	—*	● ● ●● ● ● ● ●

---

*   Seven-tone scales that exceed the octave, or fall short of the octave (which can occur by joining some tetrachords by a half step), are not classified as diatonic scales. These constructions may, however, be used in composing.

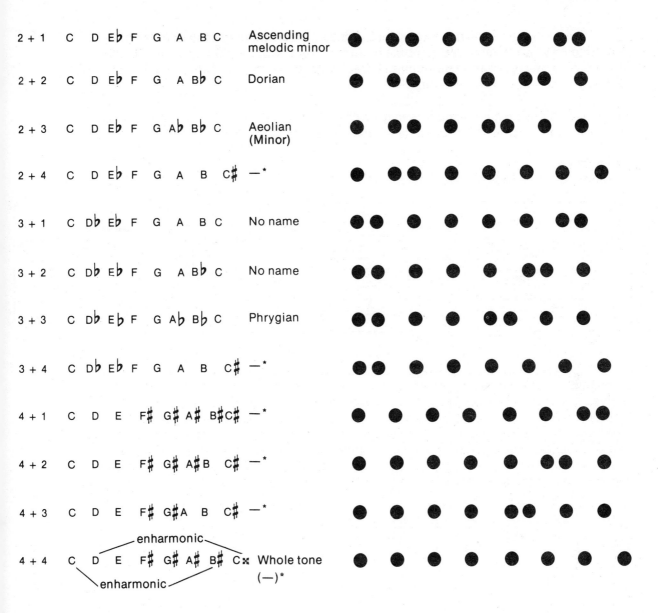

2 + 1	C D E♭ F G A B C	Ascending melodic minor
2 + 2	C D E♭ F G A B♭ C	Dorian
2 + 3	C D E♭ F G A♭ B♭ C	Aeolian (Minor)
2 + 4	C D E♭ F G A B C♯	—*
3 + 1	C D♭ E♭ F G A B C	No name
3 + 2	C D♭ E♭ F G A B♭ C	No name
3 + 3	C D♭ E♭ F G A♭ B♭ C	Phrygian
3 + 4	C D♭ E♭ F G A B C♯	—*
4 + 1	C D E F♯ G♯ A♯ B♯ C♯	—*
4 + 2	C D E F♯ G♯ A♯ B C♯	—*
4 + 3	C D E F♯ G♯ A B C♯	—*
4 + 4	C D E F♯ G♯ A♯ B♯ C𝄪	Whole tone (—)*

enharmonic

enharmonic

All of the modes are constructed by the above procedure (whole step between tetrachords) except two: the Lydian and the Locrian. Reference to Example 3.8 will show that the tetrachords of these two are joined by a half step.

Example 3.8
Two Tetrachords Joined by a Half Step

TYPE	SPELLING	SCALE NAME	DIAGRAMMATIC PATTERN
4 + 1	C D E F♯ G A B C	Lydian	
3 + 4	C D♭ E♭ F G♭ A♭ B♭ C	Locrian	

The procedure shown in Examples 3.7 and 3.8 is primarily for the purpose of illustrating how two tetrachords combine to form diatonic scales. You may wish to construct scales that result from combining tetrachords joined by a half step, in addition to the two that were shown in Example 3.8.

The following hand diagrams may be of value in the drill on tetrachords. Scales can be similarly expressed by using two hands in vertical position.

Example 3.9
Diagrammatic Symbols for Tetrachords

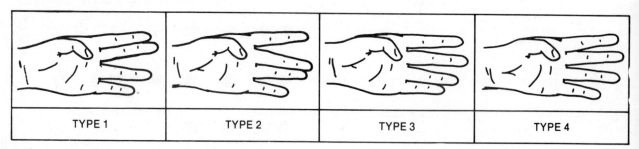

| TYPE 1 | TYPE 2 | TYPE 3 | TYPE 4 |

The next section of this chapter will discuss the two scales familiar to us through the music we hear most often: the major and minor scales. These scales are derived from two of the modes, the Ionian and the Aeolian, respectively. Before going further, however, you should be sure you know all the modes. (Refer to Example 3.1.) Learn to build them on the white keys first, then to transpose them to other tonics by keeping the identical step and half-step arrangements between scale members. Pianists as well as nonpianists may benefit in the beginning study of scales by playing the two connecting tetrachords on the piano as follows.

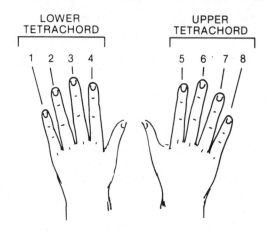

CHECK YOUR UNDERSTANDING

Chapter 3, No. 2

1. Using only the white keys of the piano keyboard, list in order the seven combinations which would be classified as tetrachords. The first is solved as an example.

   a) _____C, D, E, F_____   b) _____   c) _____

   d) _____   e) _____   f) _____

   g) _____

2. The first four tones of a scale (1,2,3,4) are called the _____ tetrachord.

3. The last four tones of a scale (5,6,7,8) are called the _____ tetrachord.

4. There are _____ types of nonduplicating diatonic tetrachords in the octave.

5. Considering only the white keys of the piano keyboard, show by the use of brackets the four types of tetrachords. (Refer to Example 3.5.)

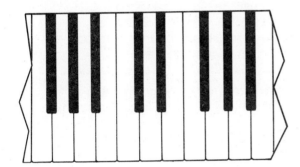

6. Considering only the white keys of the piano keyboard, show by use of diagrammatic patterns the four types of tetrachords.

   Type 1:   Type 3:

   Type 2:   Type 4:

7. A _____ scale is constructed by two properly chosen diatonic tetrachords joined by a _____ or a _____ _____ .

8. Explain why two Type 4 tetrachords joined by a whole step cannot be used to construct a diatonic scale. _____

   _____

   _____

9. Spell the tetrachord combinations shown below, starting on the given note (letter). Join the tetrachords by a whole step. Identify the mode. The first is solved as an example.

Types	Spelling								Mode
a) 1 + 1	C	D	E	F	G	A	B	C	Ionian
b) 2 + 2	D								
c) 2 + 3	A								
d) 3 + 3	E								
e) 1 + 2	G								

10. The church mode formed by joining a Type 3 tetrachord to a Type 4 tetrachord by a half step is called _____

11. The mode formed by joining a Type 4 tetrachord to a Type 1 tetrachord by a half step is called _____

12. What kind of scale results from joining a Type 4 tetrachord to a Type 4 tetrachord by a whole step? _____ _____

13. Which two tetrachords are joined by a step to form the C-major scale? Type _____ and Type _____. Spell the C-major scale.

_____

14. Spell the tetrachord combinations shown below, starting on the given note. Join the tetrachords by a whole step. Identify the mode. The first is solved as an example.

Types	Spelling								Name
a) 3 + 3	G♯	A	B	C♯	D♯	E	F♯	G♯	Phrygian
b) 1 + 1	B♭								
c) 1 + 2	B♭								
d) 2 + 2	F♯								
e) 2 + 2	B♭								
f) 1 + 1	A♭								
g) 2 + 3	E								
h) 2 + 3	F								
i) 3 + 3	A								

15. Write the following modes, ascending. Start each mode on G2. Construct by the tetrachord principle. (Refer to Examples 3.7 and 3.8.)

a) Mixolydian

(continued)

_____
(Name)

b) Ionian

c) Dorian

d) Aeolian

e) Lydian

f) Phrygian

16. Among the following, underscore only those terms or symbols that refer to _diatonic scale construction._

half step   tetrachord   tempo   diminished triad   motion
chord root   whole step   Type 1 tetrachord   interval
Dorian tetrachord   chord quality   Hz   Phrygian tetrachord
Lydian tetrachord   diatonic scale   Mixolydian mode   Dorian mode
basic triad   Lydian mode   major triad   irregular division

(Be sure you can define all of the above.)

STAFF FOR SKETCHING

MAJOR AND HARMONIC MINOR SCALES

During the 17th century, specific alterations of scale members of some of the modes resulted in a reduction of the scale constructions to two modes, the Ionian and the Aeolian. This mutation generally occured as follows.

Original Mode	Scale Member Altered	Resulting Mode
Ionian on C	none	Ionian on C
Dorian on D	lower the sixth	Aeolian on D
Phrygian on E	raise the second	Aeolian on E
Lydian on F	lower the fourth	Ionian on F
Mixolydian on G	raise the seventh	Ionian on G
Aeolian on A	none	Aeolian on A
Locrian on B	The Locrian mode was not used.	

And even the Aeolian mode was later altered. It became increasingly more common for composers to raise the seventh member of this mode, thus changing the subtonic to a leading tone. This scale became generally known as the **harmonic minor scale** and the Ionian mode as the **major scale.** These, then, were the two scale constructions favored by composers during most of the 17th, 18th, and 19th centuries. Our study will now concentrate on these scales: the **major scale** and the **harmonic minor scale**.

The Major Scale

The following statements relate to the major scale whose tonic is C.

1.   The major scale is identical in construction to the Ionian mode.

2.   It is formed from C to C on the white keys of the piano.

3.   It results from combining tetrachord Types 1 + 1 joined by a step.

4.   Its tonic is C; its dominant is G; its subdominant is F.

5.   The interval of a half step occurs between scale members 3 and 4 and between scale members 7 and 8.

6.   Scale members 1, 3, 5 form a major triad, the tonic triad.

7.   The scale is often referred to as a **major mode.** *

8.   The correct name for the scale whose tonic is C is a "C-major scale."

9.   By retaining the identical relationship of pitches, a major scale can be constructed on each of the twelve pitches. (See Example 3.15.)

10.   Music based on this scale is said to be "in the key of C," or "in the key of C major."

Example 3.2 shows a melody that is in C major as well as C Ionian.

---

*   The Ionian, Lydian, and Mixolydian modes are also referred to as major modes because their scale members 1,3,5 form a major triad. The Aeolian, Dorian, and Phrygian modes are referred to as minor modes because their scale members 1,3,5 form a minor triad.

The Harmonic Minor Scale

The following statements relate to the harmonic minor scale whose tonic is A:

1.   The harmonic minor scale is constructed the same as the Aeolian mode with a raised seventh scale member. (Compare Example 3.1(a) with Example 3.10.)

2.   It results from combining a Type 2 tetrachord with a *nondiatonic* tetrachord joined by a whole step.*

3.   Its tonic is A; its dominant is E; its subdominant is D.

4.   The interval of a half step occurs between scale members 2 and 3, 5 and 6, and 7 and 8. The interval of an augmented second occurs between scale members 6 and 7.

5.   Scale members 1,3,5 form a minor triad, the tonic triad.

6.   The scale is often referred to as a **minor mode**.†

7.   The correct name for the scale whose tonic is A is an "A harmonic-minor scale" or, more often, simply an "A-minor scale."

8.   By retaining the identical relationship of pitches, a minor scale can be constructed on each of the twelve pitches. (See Example 3.16.)

9.   Music based on this scale is said to be "in the key of A minor."

   The harmonic minor scale has been second in importance only to the major scale in Western music of the past 300 years. Musicians seemed to prefer the sound of the raised seventh. This **leading tone** produced a stronger tonality and, furthermore, resulted in a major dominant triad rather than the minor dominant of the Aeolian mode. (The change in harmony probably accounts for the name of this scale.)

Example 3.10
The Harmonic Minor Scale

   Like so many changes, the alteration of the seventh scale member produced a problem. The melodic interval of the augmented second between scale members 6 and 7 was perhaps too non-Western sounding for early European ears, and it was difficult

---

*   Although the harmonic minor scale is not, strictly speaking, a diatonic scale according to our definition, we will henceforth refer to it as one because of its *harmonic* derivation (the preference for the major dominant chord) and because the frequent avoidance of the augmented second in *melodic* writing gives it diatonic properties.

†   The Ionian, Lydian, and Mixolydian modes are also referred to as major modes because their scale members 1,3,5 form a major triad. The Aeolian, Dorian, and Phrygian modes are referred to as minor modes because their scale members 1,3,5 form a minor triad.

to sing or play in tune. This problem was solved by another alteration: the sixth scale member was raised when a line moved upward through the upper tetrachord, and the seventh scale member was lowered to its Aeolian form when the line descended through the upper tetrachord. (Sometimes this procedure was reversed.) Example 3.11 shows the ascending and descending tradition in scale form, and Example 3.12 illustrates the raised sixth member in an excerpt from Handel.

Example 3.11
The Common Alterations in the Harmonic Minor Scale*

Example 3.12
Handel, *Suite No. 10,* Allegro (Transposed to A minor)

Although composers felt free to alter the sixth and seventh scale members as they wished, the harmonic minor (without the raised sixth alteration as shown in Example 3.10) was definitely the preferred scale. The Bach melody below, transposed to A minor, illustrates the use of both the natural and the raised seventh member in the same measure.

Example 3.13
J. S. Bach, *Two-Part Inventions, No. 2*

Moderato

One other alteration was also prevalent during this period: the raising of the third scale member in the final chord, to produce a major triad. This change, which resulted in a more final sound, was called the **Picardy third** .

---

*   Most theory texts refer to this scale construction as a "melodic minor scale," but due to its limited use in music of all periods (to eliminate the interval of the augmented second) we will consider it as an altered form of the harmonic minor scale. Also, most texts refer to the later use of the Aeolian mode as the "natural minor," "normal minor," or "Aeolian minor." We prefer to refer to this construction as the Aeolian mode.

The preference for the *major* scale and the *minor* scale in the music of approximately the past 300 years did not mean that the old church modes were obsolete—they merely remained partially dormant, to reappear at a later date. The modes continued to be significant scale structures for folk music, although they were not a substantial part of art music until the Impressionistic period, around the turn of the 20th century. Impressionistic music, plus modal folk tunes, no doubt had a profound influence on pop, rock, and jazz music. The following example (in Dorian on C) illustrates one folk song that become popular with rock artists in the seventies.

Example 3.14
English Folk, "Scarborough Fair"

CHECK YOUR UNDERSTANDING

Chapter 3, No. 3

1. The two scales which came into prominence with the diminishing use of the church modes were the _____ scale and _____ _____ scale.

2. During the common practice period, the major scale and the harmonic minor scale were in popular favor. The seventh scale member of these two scales is called the _____ _____.

3. Once again, spell each of the church modes, starting on the given notes, and identify by name.

   a) A __ __ __ __ __ __ A _____

   b) B __ __ __ __ __ __ __ _____

   c) C __ __ __ __ __ __ __ _____

   d) D __ __ __ __ __ __ __ _____

   e) E __ __ __ __ __ __ __ _____

   f) F __ __ __ __ __ __ __ _____

   g) G __ __ __ __ __ __ __ _____

4. The major scale is identical in structure to the _____ mode. It combines the following two tetrachords joined by a step: Types _____ and_____

5. Scale members 1, 3, 5 of a major scale spell a _____ triad.

6. Write the C-major scale on each staff below.

7. The lower tetrachord of the minor scale is a Type _____ tetrachord.

8.   An F-major scale results when the _____ scale member of the
     Lydian mode is _____. Write this F-major scale below.

     _____
     _____
     _____
     _____
     _____

9.   Scale members 1, 3, 5 of a minor scale spell a _____ triad.

10. The minor scale form which predominated in the music of the 18th and 19th
     centuries resulted in one particular alteration from the Aeolian form: a

     _____ _____ scale member.

     Write this scale below with its tonic on A.

     _____
     _____
     _____
     _____
     _____

     This scale is called a _____ minor scale.

11. The alteration made to form the harmonic minor scale created an augmented
     second interval between scale members 6 and 7. This interval was occasionally

     eliminated by raising the _____ scale member, or by

     _____

12. Write the Aeolian mode on A on the staff below. Place correct alteration signs in
     parentheses before the two traditionally altered scale members, to show that
     these two members can be used in natural or altered form.

     _____
     _____
     _____
     _____
     _____

13. Scale members 1, 3, 5 of the Ionian mode spell a _____ triad.

14. Scale members 1, 3, 5 of the Aeolian mode spell a _____ triad.

15. Among the following, underscore only those terms or symbols that refer to
     diatonic scale construction.

     chromatic   octave   whole-tone scale   upper tetrachord
     Type 1   harmonic interval   diatonic tetrachord   unit-pattern
     lower tetrachord   C-major scale   Aeolian minor   major modes
     intensity   measure   seventh chord

     (Be sure you can define all of the above.)

TRANSPOSITION OF SCALES AND THE CIRCLE OF FIFTHS

The modes (scales) were shown in Example 3.1 in their basic (untransposed) forms. They were shown in Examples 3.7 and 3.8 **transposed** (moved) to a tonic of C. Scales can use any of the twelve tones as their tonic note. Example 3.15 (p. 128) shows the major scale spelled on all twelve notes. We start the first scale on C, the next a perfect fifth higher on G, and so on, with the upper tetrachord of one major scale becoming the lower tetrachord of the next major scale. Of course, both tetrachords are Type 1 tetrachords.

Another diagrammatic way of illustrating the spelling of major scales is by the **circle of fifths**. Example 3.16 (p. 129) shows the progression of major scales by perfect fifths: ascending fifths when moving clockwise, and descending fifths when moving counterclockwise. The minor scales are shown also, but in parentheses. The sharps, starting with F♯, are added one at a time (also in ascending fifths) when moving in the clockwise direction, and flats, starting with B♭, are added one at a time (in descending fifths) when moving in the counterclockwise direction. Study Example 3.16 carefully, for it will be useful in the understanding of key signatures, as well as in your later study of chord progression.

You will notice that the F♯-major scale is enharmonic with the G♭-major scale. The six-sharp/six-flat scale is the usual dividing point between the sharp-spelled and the flat-spelled scales.

Let us pause now to take note of the dual relationships that exist between diatonic scales: (a) we say that two diatonic scales are **related** when they share the same *tones* (C Ionian, D Dorian, E Phrygian, etc.) and (b) we say that two diatonic scales are **parallel** when they share the same *tonics* (C major, C Mixolydian, C Dorian, etc.). Traditionally, the word **relative** is used for a specific kind of relationship—the one that exists between C major and A minor, F major and D minor, etc.

To apply this understanding, look again at the circle of fifths. In Example 3.16, the relative minor scales appear in parentheses below their corresponding major scales. Note that the tonic of the relative minor scale is a minor third below the tonic of the corresponding major scale. We say that "A minor is the relative minor of C major," or that "C major is the relative major of A minor." The scales are related because the C-major scale and the A-minor scale (Aeolian form) use exactly the same tones. Actually, you might say that the C-minor scale is more closely akin to the C-major scale than is the A-minor scale, since their tonics are the same. Be that as it may, standard usage requires that we refer to C major and C minor as being "parallel" rather than "related." We say that "C major is the parallel major to C minor."

Since minor scales share the same tones as their relative majors, transposition of a minor scale is accomplished by adding sharps and flats in the same places and in the same order (by ascending or descending fifths) as for its relative major.

The circle of fifths (Example 3.16) is also useful in understanding the transposition of the modes:

a)   The basic modes shown in Example 3.1 have no sharps or flats, the same as C major and A minor.

Example 3.15
The Major Scale Spelled on All Twelve Notes

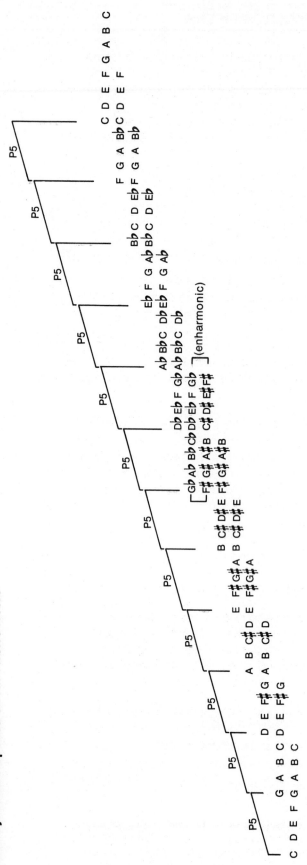

(Notice that we have moved upward in fifths until we have returned to the major scale built on C.)

Example 3.16
The Circle of Fifths*

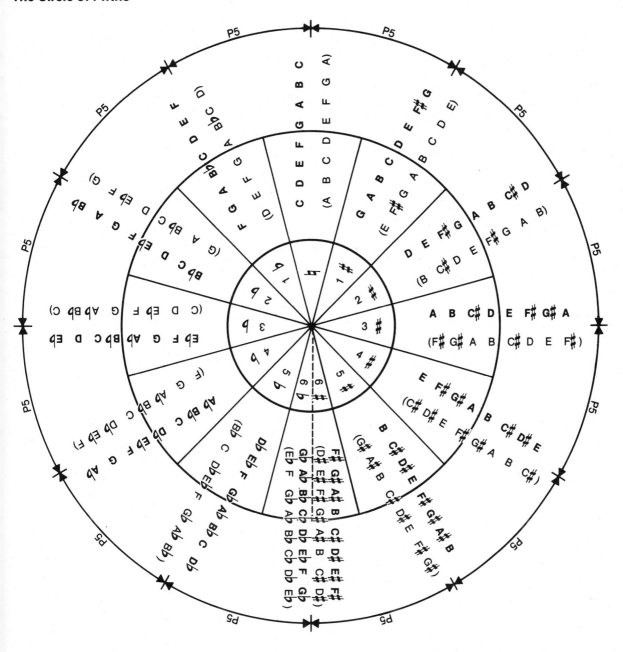

b)   When any mode is transposed up a perfect fifth from its previous form, one additional sharp is added. For example, Mixolydian on D, a perfect fifth above the basic form, would be spelled D E F♯ G A B C D. If this were transposed up another perfect fifth, to A, a second sharp would be added, here C♯. Mixolydian on A would be spelled A B C♯ D E F♯ G A, and so on.

---

*   The alteration signs above do not include the raised seventh member in the harmonic minor scale. **Key signatures**, which are discussed in the next section, will show this same incongruity—that only alteration signs for the Aeolian form are included, the raised seventh being treated as an alteration.

c)   When any mode is transposed down a perfect fifth from its previous form, one additional flat is added. For example, Mixolydian on C, a perfect fifth below its basic form, would be spelled C D E F G A B♭ C; Mixolydian on F, another fifth lower, would be spelled F G A B♭ C D E♭ F; and so on.

At this point, scales and especially their transpositions may seem formidable, but they are not. You can learn to write all diatonic scales by the tetrachord system of organization, being aware of whole- and half-step arrangements, or by a knowledge of *key signatures,* discussed in the next section. And eventually, when your ears become sufficiently accustomed to the sounds of the various scales, you will have little difficulty writing them "by ear," notating the pitches you hear inwardly.

CHECK YOUR UNDERSTANDING
Chapter 3, No. 4

1. Any of the scales discussed so far can be written starting on _____ different pitches. For example, the Dorian on D can also be started with its tonic on Eb, on E, on_____, on _____, on _____, on _____, on _____, on _____, on _____, on _____, and on _____, as well as on the enharmonic equivalents of these pitches.

2. Then the C-major scale is transposed *up* a perfect fifth, _____ sharp is needed to maintain the correct interval relationship between scale members. When it is transposed yet another perfect fifth higher, _____ more sharp must be used. The first sharp, added for the scale's transposition to G, is _____. The second sharp, added for the scale's transposition to D, is _____. Each additional sharp added, as the transpositions move up a perfect fifth, is an interval of a _____ _____ above the last sharp.

3. The D-major scale has _____ sharps: _____ and _____. The A-major scale has _____ sharps: _____ , _____ , and _____.

4. When the C-major scale is transposed *down* a perfect fifth, one _____ is needed to maintain the correct intervallic relationship between scale members. When it is transposed yet another perfect fifth lower, _____ more flat must be used. The first flat, added for the scale's transposition to F, is _____. The second flat, added for the scale's transpositon to Bb, is _____. Each additional flat added, as the transpositions move down a perfect fifth, is an interval of a _____ _____ below the last flat.

5. The F-major scale has _____ flat: _____. The Bb-major scale has _____ flats: _____ and _____. The Eb-major scale has _____ flats: _____ , _____ , and _____. The consecutive order of the first four flats spells a well-known word: _____.

6. Without referring more than once to Example 3.16, fill in the circle of fifths on the reverse side, showing only the tonic notes of the major scales and the number of sharps or flats used in each scale.

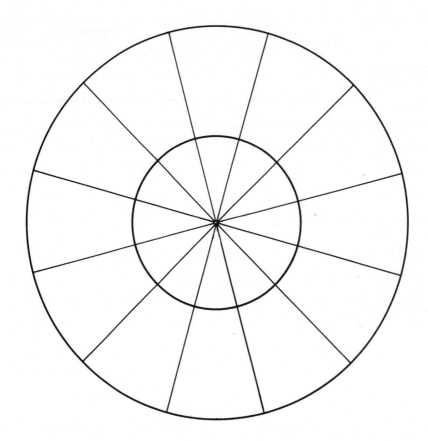

7. List the order in which sharps are added when the basic scales are transposed clockwise in the circle of fifths. The first is given.

 F♯ _____ _____ _____ _____ _____ _____ _____ *

8. List the order in which flats are added when the basic scales are transposed counterclockwise in the circle of fifths. The first is given.

 B♭ _____ _____ _____ _____ _____ _____ _____ *

9. You have noticed that the F♯-major scale is enharmonic with the G♭-major scale. Similarly, the _____ -major scale is enharmonic with the D♭-major scale, and the _____ -major scale with the B-major scale.

---

* The seventh sharp and flat are not shown in Example 3.16.

(continued)

10. When the Aeolian form of the minor scale on A is transposed _up_ a perfect fifth, _____ sharp is needed to maintain the correct intervallic relationships between scale members. When it is transposed yet another perfect fifth higher, _____ more sharp must be used. The first sharp added is _____. When the A-minor scale is transposed _down_ a perfect fifth_____ flat is needed: _____. When transposed down another perfect fifth to G, _____ more flat must be used. The two flats for G-minor are _____ and _____.

11. The relative minor of C major is_____ _____; the relative minor of F major is _____ _____; the relative minor of G major is_____ _____; the relative major of E minor is _____ _____; the relative major of C minor is _____ _____.

12. The parallel minor to A major is_____ _____; the parallel major to D minor is_____ _____.

13. You have learned that the circle of fifths can also be used in the transposition of the church modes to other tonics. Starting with the modes on the white keys, show the flats or sharps which would be required to make the following transpositions. The first is solved as an example.

					Alterations Required
a)	Aeolian on A	to	Aeolian on E		F♯ _____
b)	Aeolian on A	to	Aeolian on B		_____
c)	Aeolian on A	to	Aeolian on F♯		_____
d)	Aeolian on A	to	Aeolian on D		_____
e)	Aeolian on A	to	Aeolian on G		_____
f)	Dorian on D	to	Dorian on A		_____
g)	Dorian on D	to	Dorian on E		_____
h)	Dorian on D	to	Dorian on G		_____
i)	Dorian on D	to	Dorian on C		_____
j)	Dorian on D	to	Dorian on B♭		_____
k)	Mixolydian on G	to	Mixolydian on D		_____
l)	Mixolydian on G	to	Mixolydian on C		_____
m)	Mixolydian on G	to	Mixolydian on B		_____

14.   Write the following scales (ascending) on the staff. Place sharps or flats before the notes they alter.

    a) Aeolian on E

    b) Mixolydian on C

    c) Dorian on F

    d) D major

    e) B♭ major

    f) A♭ major

    g) B major

    h) G harmonic minor

    i) F harmonic minor

    j) E harmonic minor

    k) C harmonic minor

15.   Among the following, underscore only those terms or symbols that refer to *diatonic scales and their transposition*.

circle of fifths	fundamental	relative minor	rhythm-pattern	
unit-pattern	parallel minor	amplitude	relative major	timbre
Aeolian form	harmonics	Mixolydian on D	E-major scale	triad
Dorian on G	G Dorian	F+	minor chord	chord quality

    (Be sure you can define all of the above.)

KEY SIGNATURES

The term **key signature** refers to the practice of placing the required number of sharps or flats used in tonal music just after the clef sign and before the measure signature. These sharps and flats usually identify the scale being used in the music. The idea was that any of these notes found in the body of the music, and in any octave, would be so altered (without further use of alteration signs) unless cancelled by a natural sign.*
The term "key," as used here, means **tonality**, the condition which exists when a *key center*, or *tonic center*, dominates and assumes the position of a home tone.†

A scale, like a music composition, may be written either without a key signature (Example 3.17a) or with a key signature (Example 3.17b).

Example 3.17
E-Major Scale

a) Without Signature

b) With Signature

Some think that the key signature was more an aid to the music copyist than to the performer. As long as the music stayed in one key, the copyist was saved the labor of inserting an alteration sign before each individual note that needed one in that key. It was up to the performer to carry this information in his head as he read across the staff. But even with a key signature, when the music **modulates** (changes to a new key center), one of two procedures has to be followed: (a) the old signature has to be cancelled and a new one inserted into the body of the music (this can be cumbersome if the music changes keys often); or (b) the inappropriate notes of the original key have to be altered, sometimes throughout a long sequence of measures, to conform to those of the new key. The key signature is therefore not an entirely satisfactory solution to notational problems. But since the great majority of our tonal music *is* written with key signatures, it is necessary to understand how they function.

The appropriate sharps or flats are placed in the key signature on the required lines and spaces in a specified order. The order follows the pattern of ascending perfect fifths for sharps, starting with F♯, and the pattern of descending perfect fifths for flats, starting with B♭. (Refer to the circle of fifths in Example 3.16.) Although the *order* never changes, the *placement* of sharps and flats varies with the clef used. Example 3.18 shows the correct order and the correct placement for the treble, bass, alto, and tenor clefs. The signatures are identified according to their traditional use for major and minor tonalities.

---

*   Any alteration sign *over and beyond* those used in the key signature alters only that specific pitch (not the octave equivalent) and only within the measure. The measure barline cancels the alteration except for notes tied across the barline.

†   The subject of tonality will be discussed in more detail in Book II.

Example 3.18
Key Signatures for Major and Minor Tonalities*

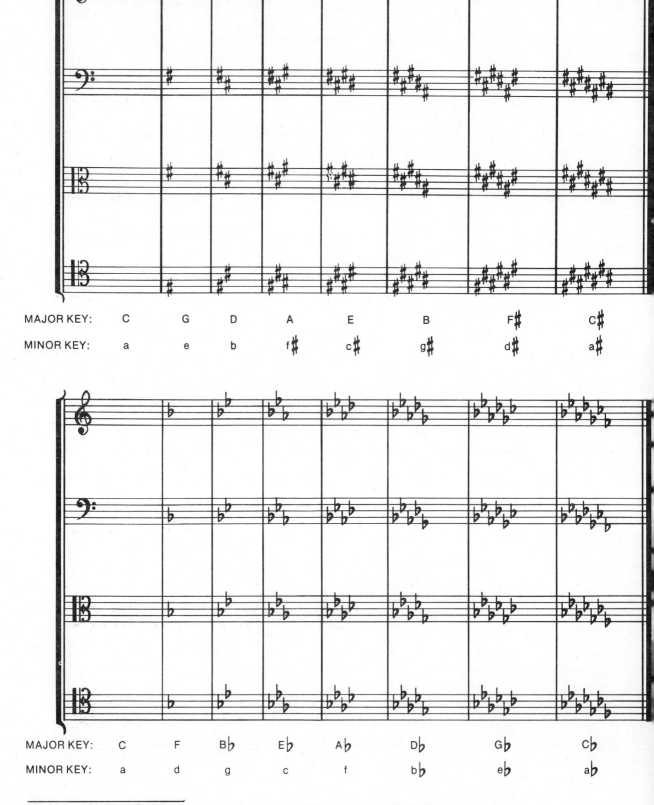

MAJOR KEY:	C	G	D	A	E	B	F♯	C♯
MINOR KEY:	a	e	b	f♯	c♯	g♯	d♯	a♯

MAJOR KEY:	C	F	B♭	E♭	A♭	D♭	G♭	C♭
MINOR KEY:	a	d	g	c	f	b♭	e♭	a♭

*   In the harmonic minor scale, the raised seventh member is treated as an alteration. Although it would be possible to do so, it is the convention never to place in the key signature the alteration sign that raises this scale member.

MODAL KEY SIGNATURES

Although the transposition of the modes can be calculated by reference to the circle of fifths, it can also be accomplished by the use of key signatures and by relating a mode to its corresponding major scale. **For this purpose only, refer to Example 3.1 and note the following.**

The Aeolian mode starts and ends on the sixth scale member of a major scale.

The Ionian mode starts and ends on the first scale member of a major scale.

The Dorian mode starts and ends on the second scale member of a major scale.

The Phrygian mode starts and ends on the third scale member of a major scale.

The Lydian mode starts and ends on the fourth scale member of a major scale.

The Mixolydian mode starts and ends on the fifth scale member of a major scale.

Applying this knowledge, one can determine that the Dorian mode on B♭ uses the same key signature as does the A♭-major scale, or to put it in the form of a proportion:

$$\frac{\text{D Dorian}}{\text{C Major}} = \frac{\text{B♭ Dorian}}{\text{A♭ Major}}$$

This is so because B♭ is the second scale member in the A♭-major scale.

In analyzing music you should be cautioned that the key signature does not always identify the tonality, because the tonality is subject to change as the music proceeds. In tonal music of all styles it is customary to use the signature of the *predominating* tonality, even though the music wanders through other keys. The final chord will usually be a tonic in the original key, and the beginning of the music will usually be in this predominant tonality. Internal sections, however, will often be in other keys, regardless of whether the signature has changed.

A further risk in identifying tonality by key signature results from a composer's use of the church modes. A signature of one flat, for example, will usually indicate a tonality of F major or D minor. However, it *could* be used as a signature for the Dorian mode on G, the Phrygian mode on A, the Lydian mode on B♭, or the Mixolydian mode on C. Also, in modal writing, a composer will often use the key signature of the mode's parallel major or minor key, for example, two flats for Dorian on G, or one sharp for Mixolydian on G. Those alteration signs that are not needed are cancelled in the body of the music.

Unfortunately, there is no universal procedure for modal signatures. The three methods are illustrated in Example 3.19 by a fragment of a folk melody, "A Virgin Most Pure," written in the Dorian mode on F.

Example 3.19
Modal Signatures

a) Without key signature

b) With the modal signature

c) With the parallel minor signature*

It is partly because of these impediments that many composers of today's tonal music do not use a key signature, but instead simply add alteration signs as required by the music.

Occasionally, when the music is not tonally complex, but uses a diatonic scale other than one of those previously named, a composer will resort to a nontraditional key signature. The following is often called the **overtone scale**.

Example 3.20
A Nontraditional Key Signature

It was said earlier that "to understand melody is to understand scales." A very large part of the music heard today can, by analysis, be reduced to one or more of the scales presented in this chapter. Not only do scales form an important structural basis for melody, but they function in a similar fashion as a structure for harmony. They must be understood thoroughly if one is to become a proficient musician.

---

*   Another example is found in Check Your Understanding, Chapter 5, No. 2, #5.

CHECK YOUR UNDERSTANDING

Chapter 3, No. 5

1. The purpose of key signatures is to _____

   _____

   _____

2. Does the sharp or flat in the signature refer just to that pitch, or to all octave

   equivalents? _____

3. Any alteration sign placed before a note in the body of the music affects

   _____

4. Name the consecutive order of the sharps as introduced in the key signature.
   The first sharp is given.

   F♯ ____ ____ ____ ____ ____ ____

5. Name the consecutive order of the flats as introduced in the key signature. The
   first flat is given.

   B♭ ____ ____ ____ ____ ____ ____

6. Do the sharps or flats follow the same order in the signature as they do in the

   circle of fifths? _____

7. Is the seventh scale member of the harmonic minor scale normally included in

   the key signature? _____

8. Write the key signatures on the grand staff as instructed, being careful to place
   the symbols precisely on the correct lines or spaces. (Bear in mind that the typical alterations that occur in minor are not shown in the key signatures.) The first
   two are solved as examples.

a) G major

b) G Minor

c) A major

d) E♭ major

e) E major

f) Ab major

(Continue, drawing sharps, flats, clef signs, braces, and vertical lines as similar as possible to the models above.)

g) B major

h) Db major

i) C# major

j) Cb major

k) E minor

l) C minor

m) C# minor

n) D minor

o) F# minor

p) F minor

9.   A mode can easily be transposed if one knows how its scale members relate to its relative major scale. Show this relationship below. The first is solved as an example.

a) The Dorian starts and ends on the _____second_____ scale member of a major scale.

(continued)

    b) The Phrygian starts and ends on the _____ scale member of a major scale.

    c) The Lydian starts and ends on the _____ scale member of a major scale.

    d) The Mixolydian starts and ends on the _____ scale member of a major scale.

    e) The Aeolian starts and ends on the _____ scale member of a major scale.

10.   Write the following modes using the appropriate *modal* key signature (Example 3.19b). The first is solved as an example.

a) Mixolydian on A

b) Dorian on C

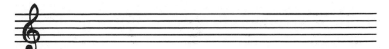

c) Dorian on E

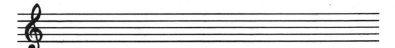

d) Mixolydian on F

e) Phrygian on B

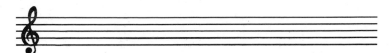

f) Lydian on E♭

g) Lydian on D

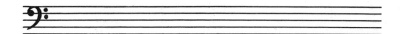

(continued)   141

h) Aeolian on F♯

i) Ionian on C♯

11.   Write the key signature of C♯ major on the alto and tenor clefs.

12.   Write the key signature of C♭ major on the alto and tenor clefs.

13.   Among the following, underscore only those terms or symbols that refer to *scales, transpositions of scales, or key signatures*.

measure signature   key signature   meter   key center   pulse
tonic center   compound intervals   tonality   accent   key of F
five-flat signature   root   modulate   rhythm   tertian chord
predominating tonality   b°

(Be sure you can define all of the above.)

Activities for Developing Music Literacy

AURAL AND KEYBOARD DRILL

1. Play and sing on neutral syllables a Type 1 tetrachord, starting on C4, until you are entirely familiar with it.

2. Given the first tone (C4), sing the Type 1 tetrachord up and down by note name (C, D, E, F, E, D, C).

3. The instructor writes on the chalkboard a Type 1 tetrachord starting on C4 and, after playing the first tone (C4), points to various notes in the tetrachord. Respond by singing pitches for the indicated notes.

4. The instructor writes four-note groups based on the Type 1 tetrachord starting on C4, then duplicates these drills and distributes them to the students.

Model

The instructor plays each group, playing one tone in each group differently than notated. Upon hearing each group, place a check mark over the note incorrectly played. (This is a drill in error detection. Instructor should check for accurate response.)

5. The instructor writes several examples of three notes of a Type 1 tetrachord starting on C4, with space allowed for the addition of the fourth note, then duplicates and distributes.

Model

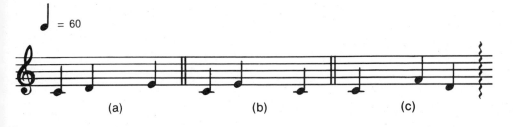

The instructor plays each example, supplying any one tone of the tetrachord to complete the four-note series. Complete the notation by inserting the note played. (Instructor should check for accurate response.)

6.   After playing C4 for tonal orientation, the instructor plays four-note groups based on the Type 1 tetrachord starting on C4. Write notes on the staff corresponding to tones played. (Instructor should check for accurate response.)

7.   Repeat Drills 4-6 starting on one of the other three tones.

8.   Repeat Drills 4-7, but use other Type 1 tetrachords.

9.   Repeat Drills 1-8 using a Type 2 tetrachord.

10.   Repeat Drills 1-8 using a Type 3 tetrachord.

11.   Repeat Drills 1-8 using a Type 4 tetrachord.

12.   Repeat any of the above drills using groups of *more* than four notes, but still limited to the tones of one of the tetrachords.

13.   Repeat Drill 12 using pulses, divisions, ties between pulses, and rests. Measure signatures should be indicated.

Model (Type 1 Tetrachord on F4)

Instructor plays and student writes:

(Sing the tetrachord before the start of dictation.)

14.   Play major scales starting on any tone. Use the fingering shown in the drawing on page 116. Notice the kind of lower tetrachord and the kind of upper tetrachord used in forming this scale. Notice that the two tetrachords are joined by a whole step. Notice where the half steps occur.

15.   Given the first tone on an instrument, sing major scales from any tone. In your drill use both numbers (1, 2, 3, 4, 5, 6, 7, 8, 7, 6, 5, 4, 3, 2, 1) and the precise note name (for example, B♭, C, D, E♭, F, G, A, B♭, A, G, F, E♭, D, C, B♭).

16.   Use the major scale for drill in the same way as the tetrachord was used in Drill 3.

17.   Use the major scale in the same way as the tetrachord was used in Drill 4. (This drill should employ primarily melodic movement by seconds, with some movement by thirds. When a reasonable proficiency is attained, more of the larger intervals can be used.)

18.   The instructor plays a major scale on a given note for tonal orientation and then plays short melodies in the same scale for dictation. (These should be played slowly and repeated as required.) You should recognize the tones being played and immediately write them on the staff. Simple folk songs in major can be

used and broken into small formal groups for dictation. These dictation exercises can be given with a note to each pulse, or in rhythm with the appropriate measure signature.

Note: This kind of dictation can extend over the entire year or longer, as proficiency is attained at each level of difficulty. But it is imperative that dictation start with exercises that are short and within the competence of all students. **The following procedure for taking melodic-rhythmic dictation will insure better results in beginning work.**

a) Instructor establishes tonal orientation by playing a scale up and down. Instructor establishes pulse rate. Instructor may or may not give the measure signature.

b) Instructor plays in tempo.

c) Student sings melody and conducts beats.

d) Instructor plays.

e) Student writes dots on lines or spaces to indicate pitch:

(Space according to duration of tone.)

f) Instructor plays.

g) Student checks for tonal accuracy.

h) Instructor plays while student conducts beats.

i) Student places check marks above notes that occur on beats:

j) Instructor plays.

k) Student decides on measure signature and changes checks to numbers:

l) Student places measure bars before each first beat, then beams all unit divisions together if appropriate:

m) Student decides on correct rhythmic notation:

n) Instructor plays.

o) Student checks for accuracy.

As you acquire more facility in dictation, many of the above steps can be combined. Eventually, all steps will be combined into one as you visualize the written page upon hearing the sounds. This drill is referred to as melodic-rhythmic dictation.

19.   Using various sources,* sing melodies based on major scales. Play the scale used for tonal orientation, then sing the melodies in tempo, using numbers or note names. Occasionally neutral syllables, such as "lah," or any other singing response may be used for vocalizing. This drill, referred to as "music reading" or "sight singing," helps develop your music literacy. Sight singing ability comes only with much practice.

20.   Apply Drills 17-19 to dictation and music reading using the harmonic minor scale and the modes.

21.   Drill on **diatonic melodic intervals** will improve your ability in sight singing and dictation, and a study of scale construction will aid you in interval identification. It is especially helpful to learn the intervals which occur above the tonic of the major scale. In the first model, sing both with scale numbers (1-1, 1-2) and with interval names (P1 = per-fect prime; M2 = ma-jor sec-ond, etc.)

Models

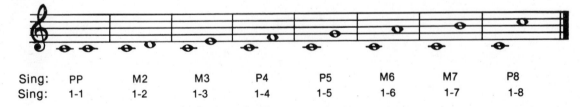

Sing:	PP	M2	M3	P4	P5	M6	M7	P8
Sing:	1-1	1-2	1-3	1-4	1-5	1-6	1-7	1-8

Notice that all of the intervals are either perfect or major. Learn to identify the following major intervals by reference to the major scale.

---

*   See Appendix 3 for a listing of source materials in sight singing.

M2: Think 1 to 2 in a major scale.

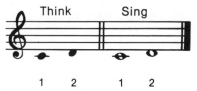

M3: Think 1 to 3 in a major scale.

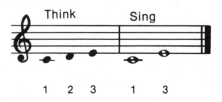

M6: Think 1 to 6 in a major scale.

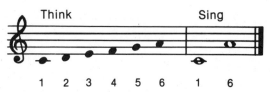

M7: Think 1 to 7 in a major scale.

Follow the above procedure to identify the perfect fourth, perfect fifth, and perfect octave.

22. With reference now to the Aeolian form of the minor scale, follow the procedure illustrated in Drill 21 to help in the identification of the minor third, minor sixth, and minor seventh.

23. Another method in interval identification associates intervals to the first two tones (not counting repetitions or grace notes) of well-known melodies.* Hopefully you will know at least one melody in each classification shown below or will locate others.

Minor second down: Donaldson, "At Sundown"; Franck, *Symphony in D Minor*, Movement I, Introduction and Theme 1; Harrison, "Something"; Rimsky-Korsakoff, *Tsar Saltan*, "Flight of the Bumble Bee"; Mozart, *Symphony No. 40*, Movement I, Theme 1

Minor second up: Beethoven, *Symphony No. 9* ("Ode to Joy"), Movement IV, Theme 1; Berlin, "White Christmas"; Dixon and Henderson, "Bye, Bye Blackbird"; Hupfield, "As Time Goes By"; Johnson and Mellish, "Drink to Me Only With Thine Eyes"

Major second down: Beethoven, *Piano Sonata No. 3 in C*, Op. 2, No. 3, Movement I, Theme 1; David and Bacharach, "Alfie"; Gerard and Armstrong, "Sweet Adeline"; Razaf and Waller, "Honeysuckle Rose"; Sibelius, *Symphony No. 2 in D*, Op. 43, Movement I, Theme 1

---

*   The themes of most of the art music examples can be found in Harold Barlow and Sam Morgenstern, *A Dictionary of Musical Themes* (New York: Crown Publishers, 1948). See Appendix 3 for source material for jazz, rock, pop, and folk music.

Major second up: Beethoven, *Piano Sonata in C Minor* ("Pathétique") Op. 13, Movement I, Introduction; Berlin, "Always"; Gruber, "Silent Night"; Lennon and McCarthy, "Eleanor Rigby"

Minor third down: Burke and Garner, "Misty"; Davis and Akst, "Baby Face"; Dett, "Juba Dance"; Key, "Star Spangled Banner"

Minor third up: Brahms, *Symphony No. 2 in D*, Op. 73, Movement I, Theme 1; Bricusse and Newley, "Candy Man"; Fields and McHugh, "Don't Blame Me"; Hanson, *Merry Mount Suite*, Theme 2; Hoffman, Livingston, and Lampl, "Close to You"

Major third down: Austin and Bergere, "How Come You Do Me Like You Do?"; Bach, *Partita No. 1*, Minuet I; Beethoven, *Symphony No. 5 in C minor*, Movement I, Theme 1; Heyward and Gershwin, "Summer Time"; Afro-American Spiritual, "Swing Low"; Strauss, *Till Eulenspiegels Lustige Streiche,* Op. 28, Theme 1

Major third up: Beethoven, *Piano Sonata in E♭* (Eroica), Op. 55, Movement I, Theme 1; Foster, "Old Black Joe"; Haydn, *Symphony No. 94 in G* ("Surprise", Movement II; Mozart, *Symphony No. 40 in G Minor*, Movement III, Theme 1; Rogers and Hammerstein, "If I Loved You"

Perfect fourth down: Beethoven, *Piano Sonata No. 18 in E♭*, Op. 31, No. 3, Movement I, Theme 1; Brahms, *Symphony No. 3 in F*, Op. 90, Movement I, Theme 2; Handel, *Messiah*, "Hallelujah Chorus"; Kalmar and Ruby, "Three Little Words"; Simons and Marks, "All of Me"

Perfect fourth up: Copland, *Appalachian Spring*, "The Gift to be Simple"; Gordon and Warren, "You'll Never Know"; Kusik and Rota, "Speak Softly, Love"; Murray, "Away in a Manger"; Prokofieff, *Peter and the Wolf*, Cat Theme

Note: Intervals of the **tritone** (augmented fourths and diminished fifths) occur considerably less often in tonal music.

Augmented fourth down: Carpenter, *String Quartet in A Minor*, Movement I, Theme 2

Augmented fourth up: Malipiero, *Impressioni Dal Vero*, Theme 1; Saint-Säens, *Concerto in C Minor for Cello and Orchestra*, Movement I, Theme 1; Sondheim and Bernstein, "Maria," from *West Side Story*

Diminished fifth down: Bartok, *Quartet No. 2*, Op. 17, Introduction, Movement II; Beethoven, *Sonata No. 19 in G Minor*, Op. 49, No. 1, Movement I, Theme 2; Mozart, *Symphony No. 29 in A*, K201, Movement I, Theme 2

Diminished fifth up: Beethoven, *Symphony No. 6 in F* ("Pastoral"), Movement IV, Theme 1; Schumann, *Carnival* for Piano, Op. 9, "Valse Noble"

Augmented fifth up: Tchaikovsky, *Symphony No. 1*, Op. 13, Movement II, Theme 1

Perfect fifth down: Delius, *In a Summer Garden*, Theme 2; Rogers and Hart, "Have You Met Miss Jones?"; Still, *Afro-American Symphony*, Movement I,

Theme 1; Terris and Robledo, "Three O'Clock in the Morning"; Tchaikovsky, *Swan Lake Suite*, Op. 20a, Movement I, Introduction

Perfect fifth up: Harris, *Symphony No. 3*, Fugue Theme; Joplin, "Maple Leaf Rag"; Magidson and Oakland, "Twinkle, Twinkle Little Star"; Mercer and Mancini, "Moon River"; Wagner, Götterdämmerung, Theme 3 (Horn)

Minor sixth down: Haydn, *String Quartet in G,* Op. 77, No. 1, Movement II; Gilbert and Ory, "Muskat Ramble"; Moussorgsky, *Pictures at an Exposition,* Theme 1, "The Gnome"; Schubert, *Symphony No. 5 in b* , Movement I, Introduction; Tchaikovsky, *Romeo and Juliet*, Theme 3

Minor sixth up: Cahn, Chaplin, and Secunda, "Bei Mir Bist Du Schön"; Hebb, "Sunny"; Shostakovich, *Symphony No. 5*, Op. 47, Movement I, Theme 1; Wagner, *Tristan und Isolde*, Prelude, Theme 1

Major sixth down: Cohan, "Over There"; Hamm, Bennett, Lown, and Gray, "Bye Bye Blues"; Koehler and Arlen, "Between the Devil and the Deep Blue Sea"; Afro-American Spiritual, "Nobody Knows the Trouble I've Seen"; Turk and Ahlert, "Mean to Me"

Major sixth up: Fuller, "Bring Back My Bonnie to Me"; Mercer and Mancini, "Days of Wine and Roses"; Olcott, "My Wild Irish Rose"; Robin, Whiting, and Harling, "Beyond the Blue Horizon"; Russell and Barroso, "Brazil"

Note: Intervals greater than the sixth occur considerably less often in tonal music.

Minor seventh down: Bruckner, *Overture in G Minor*, Theme 3; Grieg, *Papillon*, Op. 43, No. 1 for Piano; Rubenstein, *Concerto No. 4 in D Minor*, Op. 70, Movement I, Theme 2

Minor seventh up: Bernstein, "Somewhere," from *West Side Story*; Lisbona and Fine, "Today, Tomorrow and Forever"; Liszt, *Hungarian Rhapsody No. 15 in A Minor*, Theme 4; Prokofieff, *Concerto No. 1 for Violin and Orchestra*, Op. 19, Movement III, Theme 2; Schubert, *String Quartet No. 15 in G*, Op. 161, Movement II

Major seventh down: Liszt, *Faust Symphony*, Movement I, Theme 2; Ravel, *La Valse*, Theme 4

Major seventh up: Honegger, *Concertino for Piano and Orchestra*, Movement I, Theme 3; Wolf, *Italian Serenade*, Theme 2

Perfect octave down: Kahn and Donaldson, "Love Me or Leave Me"; Moussorgsky, *Pictures at an Exposition*, "Ballet of Unhatched Chickens"; Porter, "It's DeLovely"; Rachmaninoff, *Symphony No. 2 in E Minor,* Op. 27, Movement II, Theme 1

Perfect octave up: Gillespie and Coots, "You Go to My Head"; Harburg and Arlen, "Over the Rainbow"; Rose, Harburg, and Arlen, "It's Only a Paper Moon"; Washington and Harline, "When You Wish Upon a Star"; Walsh, "Christmas Story"

ANALYTICAL LISTENING

1. "Psalm 8," *The History of Music in Sound*. London: Oxford University Press; RCA Victor Records.

    "Psalm 8" is representative of early Jewish music. The melody is based on one of the four tetrachords. Which one?

2. The following melodies contain beginnings largely following the contour of the major scale. After listening to them, try to write them on manuscript paper, using correct tonality and rhythm.

    a) Beethoven, *Symphony No. 1*, Movement IV, Theme 1. Performed by the Halle Orchestra conducted by John Barbarolli, Vanguard Records SRV 146SD.

    b) Handel, *Messiah*, "Pastoral Symphony." Performed by the Philadelphia Orchestra conducted by Eugene Ormandy, Columbia Records M2S-607.

    c) Rogers and Hammerstein, *The Sound of Music*, "Do-Re-Mi." Performed by the London Cast, RCA Records LSO-2005.

    d) Stravinsky, *Concerto for Piano and Wind Instruments*. Performed by Stephen Bishop and the BBC Symphony Orchestra conducted by Colin Davis, Philips Records 839761.

    e) Tchaikovsky, *Symphony No. 4 in F Minor*, Op. 36, Movement IV, Theme 2. Performed by the Pittsburgh Symphony conducted by William Steinberg, Sine Qua Non Records 7741.

3. "Gregorian Chant," *2,000 Years of Music*, Folkway Records, FT 3700A.

    Listen to the Gregorian chant sung by men's voices from this collection. What mode do you hear? (Caution! An alteration occurs!) This type of music was typical of that performed in the church around the time of Gregory the Great, pope from 590 to 604.

4. The following melodies are based primarily on one of the diatonic modes. Try to identify the mode by ear as well as by analysis.

    a) "Nine Hundred Miles" (Folk).

    b) "God Rest Ye Merry Gentlemen" (Carol).

    c) Bach, "Aus Tiefer Not Schrei' Ich Zu Dir," from *Cantata No. 38*. (Although the melody is modal, the harmony is influenced by the major-minor harmonic system. Analyze the melody only.)

    d) "We Three Kings of Orient Are" (Carol).

    e) Chopin, "Mazurka," Op. 41, No. 1.

    f) Marlow and Scott, "A Taste of Honey."

    g) "Old Joe Clark" and "Drunken Sailor" (Folk). See Arthur Frackenpohl, *Harmonization at the Piano* (Dubuque: Wm. C. Brown Company Publishers, 1972.)

    h) Barlow, *Rhapsody for Oboe and Strings: The Winter's Past*. Performed by the Eastman-Rochester Orchestra conducted by Howard Hanson, Eastman-Rochester Archives Record 1001.

    i) "The Virgin Most Pure" (Carol). See *Oxford Book of Carols* (London: Oxford University Press, 1964).

    j) Lennon and McCartney, "Yesterday," *Yesterday...and Today.* Performed by The Beatles, Capitol Records ST-2553. (Notice how this melody moves from major to minor and vice versa. Notice how scale members 6 and 7 are used when minor tonality is implied.)

For other selections making use of modes, see Vincent Perdichetti, *Twentieth Century Harmony* (New York: W. W. Norton & Co., Inc., 1961), pages 41-42.

5. Legrand, "What Are You Doing The Rest of Your Life?" *The Way We Were*. Performed by Barbara Streisand, Columbia Records PCQ-32801.

    A good example of recent harmonic minor scale usage is found in the beginning of this tune.

6. Find other examples illustrating mostly scalewise passages (major or minor scales, or modes) from various kinds of music.

7. Study and play the short piano pieces in Bela Bartok's *Mikrokosmos*, Vol. I (New York: Boosey & Hawkes, 1940). These easy, two-part pieces may also be used for music reading and dictation.

8. Riley, *In C*. Performed by The Center of the Creative & Performing Arts, State University of Buffalo conducted by Terry Riley, Columbia Records MS 7178.

    This is a contemporary use of the C-major scale. It displays a considerable amount of **indeterminacy**, freely using over 50 isolated and repeated configurations based on diatonic tetrachords and smaller **pitch sets** from the scale. The result is more complex than one might imagine.

IMPROVISATION

1. Improvise melodies based on each one of the four tetrachords. These melodies may be doubled at the octave or double octave if played on the keyboard. Do not limit your improvisation to only those tetrachords on the white keys.

2. Improvise as above, but on major scales.

3. Improvise on the harmonic minor scale. Experiment with the use of the raised sixth.

4. Improvise on the various modes.

5. Play the **ostinato*** below while a second student improvises above it. Use only tones of a Type 2 tetrachord on D. Use a conductor.

Model (Based on a Type 2 Tetrachord)

(continued)

---

*   An **ostinato** is a melodic and/or rhythmic configuration persistently repeated—usually at the same pitch and in the lower part as an accompaniment.

6.   Produce your own ostinato through improvisation. Use notes from any one of the four tetrachord types. A second student improvises, as in Improvisation 5, on the same tetrachord.

7.   Proceed as before but use three performers, one on an ostinato and two improvising (preferably in a medium and a high register) on the same tetrachord. Use a conductor.

8.   Experiment with a bass ostinato on a Type 2 tetrachord on D and an improvisation on a Type 2 tetrachord on A. This is a simple kind of dual tonality. Also, the combined tetrachords form a Dorian mode.

9.   Experiment with other tetrachord combinations.

CREATIVE WRITING

1.   On one of the tetrachords, write a short composition in two parts for voices: a male voice on an ostinato of your choice and a female voice on an upper part. Always try your ideas at the keyboard before committing them to final form. A text may be used, with the ostinato repeating an important phrase of the text, or nontextual vocal sounds can be used throughout. Compose a third part for percussion, if you wish, or you may let the percussionist improvise. Prepare for performance. Record and replay for class evaluation.

2.   Write a short composition, similar to Improvisation 5, for voices, piano, or other instruments.

3.   Write a short composition similar to Improvisation 6.

4.   Write a short composition similar to Improvisation 7 or 8.

5.   Those more interested in contemporary techniques might wish to write a short and somewhat easier work patterned after Terry Riley's *In C* for any number of instruments. (See Analytical Listening 8. The score is supplied with the recording.) You might wish to perform a part of this work in class.

Chapter 4

Form

Form for the Creator; Form for the Performer; Form for the Listener

One of the chief charms of the musical art is the importance of the time dimension. Among the **temporal arts**—drama, dance, cinema, and music—only music uses tone as its medium of expression. The perception, coding, processing, and storage of sound stimuli present special problems to human beings. It appears to be more difficult to deal with sound events as opposed to visual events. The problem of time coupled with that of sounds makes it necessary that creators of music events exercise special care in organizing the material of a composition. The parameter involved is that of **form**.

Form is the organizational structure of music, the composer's arrangement and development of musical ideas into meaningful designs. In this sense, form is process, or growth. Some writers are struck by what appears to be the inevitability of form—by the prophetic nature of original **musical gestures** which grow into a total piece of music. And indeed, the very nature of the first, basic musical idea often does shape the design of the whole composition. Form thus grows from the inherent nature of the music itself.

From the perspective of the finished composition, form provides a kind of content **balance** in a piece of music. This balance is achieved for the most part by a blend of **unity** and **variety** that in turn stems from the composer's two most important forming tools: the restatement and contrast of music materials. The composer must consider the number and kinds of restatements, as well as the amount and degree of contrast. These factors confer shape and design on music that would otherwise be nonunified.

On the one hand, then, form refers to a process, while on the other it refers to the product or outcome. Many scholarly books are available on the subject of form, and most of them classify music by certain traditional categories of form that bear distinct labels. Among these labels of form are **binary** (two-part form), **ternary** (three-part form), **rondo, sonata-allegro,** and others too numerous to mention at this time.

Regardless of what set of labels is used, the notion of grouping compositions according to prescribed rules of restatement, contrast, resting points, and other events within the music presents many analytical problems. The beginning music student soon realizes that few compositions neatly fit into one of the molds that have enjoyed traditional designation. At the elementary level, we should focus more attention on *how the composer forms* the music, rather than on how the finished product might be classified according to textbook definitions. Although some composers select a formal mold in advance and fill it with a collection of musical ideas, the final, overall form is usually dictated largely by the initial musical ideas of the composer. Strictly speaking, the outcome is peculiar to that single piece of music only. It is true that composers through the years in all kinds of music have tended to use a relatively small number of basic design-schemes. This may be seen as simply the consequence of the state of the art at a given time; that is, the patterns that emerged reflect the order and sequence in which composers most often seemed to find their compositions culminating. In this sense the classification of "forms" is of some historical interest. But it is the "forming" process that is significant to us in our present study.

FORM FOR THE CREATOR

The composer is responsible for arranging the events within a composition in such a way that the result has aesthetic balance. This problem has always been solved by the process of restatement and contrast. It is usually desirable to incorporate some restatement, either exactly or with varying degrees of contrast (to avoid boredom), because this helps the listener to organize his or her perception of sounds into meaningful wholes by the use of memory and expectation. On the basis of what has been perceived, the listener tends to predict what is to come and thereby orders the chain of perceptions into the artistic whole intended by the composer. On the other hand, a composer must constantly be aware of the need for variety without losing control over the necessary unifying factors.

A clear grasp of the form of a piece of music is important no matter what kind of interaction with the music takes place: creating, performing, or listening. But the composer is closest of all to form. There can be no art without form or organization. The composer must realize the full organizational potential of a given set of musical ideas to create music that has balance. This is a slow painstaking process for most composers. At best, the composer may have only a kind of overall view of the composition in mind at the start of the creative effort. Similarly, the finest improvisers are able to perceive a kind of total view as they begin the instant creative process.

Simply stated, when the composer has presented an initial musical idea (usually in the form of a melodic **configuration***—but it can be rhythmic and/or harmonic) what happens next is the first semblance of the growing form. The composer can repeat the idea exactly or present different but usually related material. Clearly a wide range of choice is available, subject to the discretion of the composer. One way of thinking about these options is presented in Example 4.1.

Example 4.1
First Steps to Form: The Restatement/Contrast Continuum

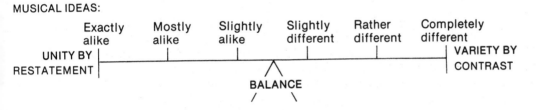

As the example implies, the composer uses restatement for unity and contrast for variety. The objective is to achieve formal balance somewhere between the two extremes. The broad range of the restatement/contrast continuum is achieved by manipulating the various parameters of music other than form: rhythm, melody, harmony, and color. Naturally, pure restatement means just that—exactly repeating an already stated musical idea; but we speak of restatement here in the broadest sense to include repetition with change.

As the element of contrast increases, the composer may choose to vary the original statement to an increasing degree. That is, to maintain unity, every event cannot be one of severe contrast, so there must be restatement; but exact repetition soon produces boredom among listeners. The notion of balance between the two extremes soon becomes clear. Compositions that possess balance are organized in such a way as to reconcile the two extremes. Naturally, it is desirable for the composer to give rein to imagination, but inventiveness must be tempered with a highly skilled technique and a sense of proportion and artistic appropriateness. The successful composer knows when just the right mixture of restatement and contrast has been attained.

---

*   A *configuration* in music is a small, self-contained unit of form constituting a germ idea; often it appears as an initial gesture encompassing anything from two tones to several measures.

Contrasting musical ideas are those that are perceived as different. Although they sound different, very often they are derived from an already stated configuration. Compare the pitch order of Example 4.2(a) with that of Example 4.2(b).

Example 4.2

a) Pitch order in $\frac{3}{4}$

b) Same pitch order in $\frac{6}{8}$

The manipulation of rhythm produces the differences in these two otherwise similar examples. Compare also "Seventy-Six Trombones" with "Goodnight My Someone," both from *The Music Man* by Meredith Willson. The similarity extends throughout!

By changing more and more of each parameter, the composer strays further and further from the original configuration. In the extreme, every aspect of the configuration may be changed. Since listeners can be led to the conclusion of contrast by very subtle changes in configurations, the extremes should be used with care. A composition that is too full of variety and nonderived contrast lacks unity, and the listeners or performers simply cannot assimilate all of the material. For this reason, such compositions become tedious to listen to, being similar in their effect to paintings, sculptures, or buildings with an excessive number of unrelated shapes, lines, and design elements.

Variants of a Configuration and Its Segments

The process of restatement with variation can be helpfully demonstrated by the use of visual analogies. We will start with a *visual* configuration, and translate this into a melody approximately conforming to the contour of the visual configuration—a melodic-rhythmic configuration.

Example 4.3
The Melodic-Rhythmic Translation of a Visual Configuration

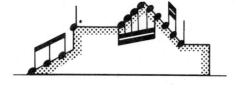 

Example 4.4 shows an original configuration and its three basic **variants**—all of which may be used within the concept of restatement. (Notice the abbreviations used.)

Example 4.4
The Three Basic, Derived Forms of the Original

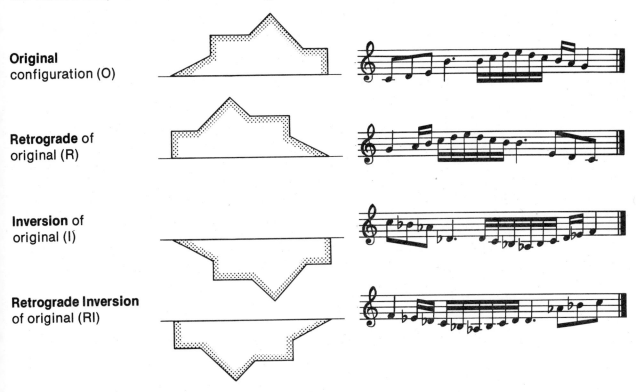

Original
configuration (O)

Retrograde of
original (R)

Inversion of
original (I)

Retrograde Inversion
of original (RI)

Observe that in the inversion and retrograde inversion, alteration signs had to be used to exactly complement the interval. This type of inversion, where *specific* intervals are used (a major second up becomes a major second down), is called a **real inversion**. Where *general* intervals are used to maintain the same scale structure (C major here), the inversion is called a **tonal inversion**. A tonal inversion would result if the alteration signs in Example 4.4 were omitted.

Many configurations (cf) can be divided into two or more segments (s). A **segment*** is a small part of a configuration used by the composer in the process of musical development to achieve both unity and variety. Our configuration divides logically into four small segments, although Segment 2 has neither sufficient rhythmic nor melodic interest to function independently.

Example 4.5
The Relation of Segments to the Configuration

---

*   The configuration and the segment are musically illustrated and defined more completely in Book II.

Other segments can be built by various combinations of these four. Many of the possibilities are shown in Example 4.6.

Example 4.6
The Division of the Configuration into Segments

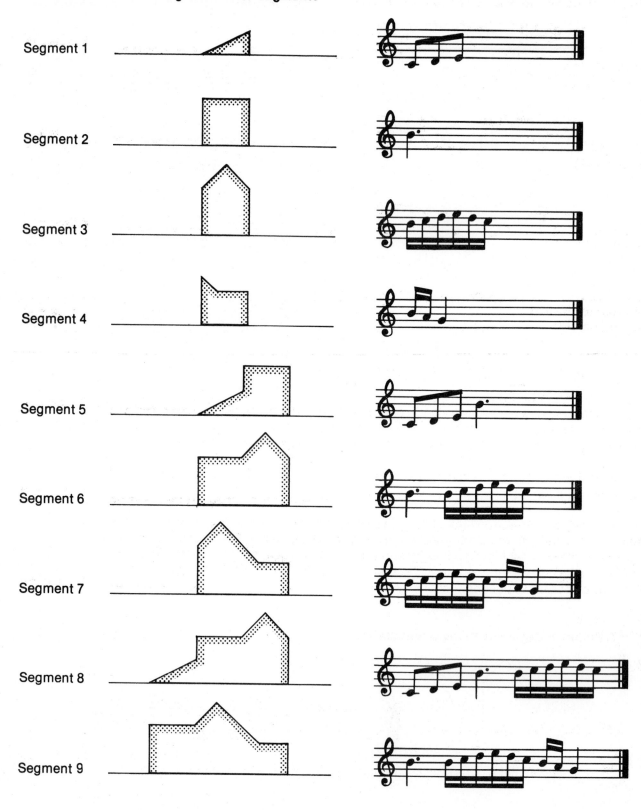

Even more patterns can be obtained by combining segments in a new order (permutation), for example 1 + 4:

Segment 10

The examples that follow illustrate other ways in which configurations and segments can retain their identity while undergoing some degree of transformation. For instance, they may be varied by **augmentation** (A), which means increasing the durational value of one or more elements in the configuration or segment; or by **diminution** (D), which means decreasing the durational value of one or more elements.

Example 4.7
The Augmentation of Segment 5

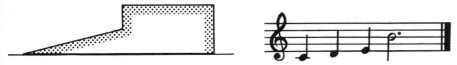

Example 4.8
The Diminution of Segment 5

Another means by which configurations can be varied is by transposition, in other words, by restatement at a different level. Immediate restatement at a different level produces a **sequence** (Seq).

Example 4.9
The Sequential Restatement of Segment 5

In music, the sequence is usually a restatement at the interval of a second or third above or below. As with an inversion (Example 4.4), a sequence may be a **real sequence** or a **tonal sequence**. The sequence in Example 4.9 is a tonal sequence, conforming to the diatonic tones of C major.

Configurations and sequences can also be varied by the **expansion** (E) or the **contraction** (C) of one or more intervals.

Example 4.10
The Vertical Variation of an Interval in Segment 5

a) By expansion:

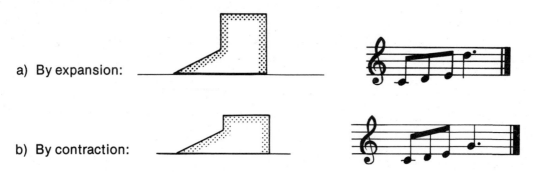

b) By contraction:

The ways of varying seem to be never-ending! The last means of varying a configuration or segment that we will discuss in this book is the **interpolation** (Int) or **deletion** (Del) of tones within a previously stated configuration or segment. This process inserts additional tones or withdraws tones from the original.

Example 4.11
The Deletion of Tones in Segment 5

Example 4.12
The Interpolation of Tones in Segment 5

Any of the above segments may also be varied by the use of retrograde and inversions (see Example 4.4); but be aware that varied restatement by use of these forms is not so common in tonal music. The means of variation illustrated in Examples 4.6 through 4.12 are more characteristic.

Keep in mind also that any of the variants above can incorporate minor rhythmic changes. And, of course, any of them can be transposed to any pitch, with the *tonal* variants being preferred for music based on the diatonic scales. Finally, a composer might select a different grouping of tones derived from our configuration.

One final example makes use of many of the processes of restatement shown in the preceding examples. Let us look at the following procession of visually related events, all variants of the original configuration.

Example 4.13
A Procession of Visually Related Events Based on Various Processes of Variation

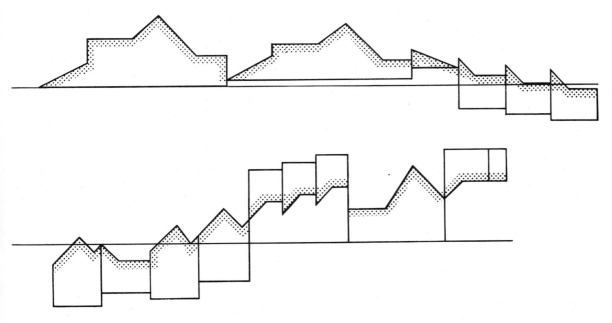

Since a part is related to its whole, it follows that we can put together a procession of segments, as well as forms derived from the original configuration, to make a pattern of sounds that has the properties of both unity and variety. Example 4.14 is an approximate translation of Example 4.13 into music notation. Compare the two versions with each other. (The abbreviations used are: O = Original; Seq = Sequence; C = Contracted; T = Transposed; R = Retrograde; I = Inversion; D = Diminution; and S1, S2, etc. refers to segment number.)

Example 4.14
Translation of Example 4.13 into Music Notation

All of the above examples should be played and compared, one with the other, in order to determine what differences and similarities exist. They can be sung, played on pitched instruments, or performed on nonpitched percussion instruments such as temple blocks, tom-toms, woodblocks, or any series of relative high-low sounds that would approximate the melodic contour. By the manipulation of these variants during improvisation and creative writing, one can readily see the extent to which creativity can be enriched by this kind of tonal thinking. However, talented composers do not restrict themselves to such a mechanistic approach as we have adopted to illustrate this technique.

CHECK YOUR UNDERSTANDING

Chapter 4, No. 1

1. Define form in your own words_____

_____

_____

_____

_____

2. Supply the opposites for the given terms below.

a) restatement _____ b) unity _____

3. List as many items relating to form as you can think of that a composer must consider in writing a piece of music.

_____

_____

_____

_____

_____

_____

_____

_____

_____

_____

4. List the three basic, derived forms of an original configuration.

_____ , _____ , _____ _____

5. Using the given visual configuration, draw the three basic, derived forms.* The original is given.

---

* Many kinds of configurations can be easily drawn with the aid of a template such as the Martin Pickett, No. 1053.

6.   Isolate and draw each of the identified segments. Also draw two larger seg-
      ments 1 + 2 and 2 + 3.

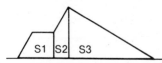

7.   Draw the three basic, derived forms of Segment 3. First, show the original seg-
      ment.

8.   Draw a procession of visually related events based on the configuration and its
      segments. Label each segment. (Refer to Examples 4.5 and 4.6.)

9.   In the procession below, which configuration or segment appears to offer *ex-
      cessive* contrast for such a short series of events? Number _____

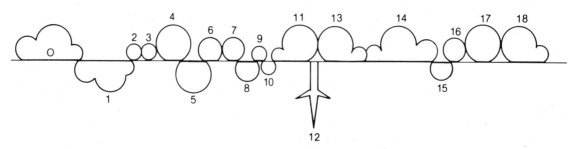

10.   Using the given configuration as a model, draw a descending sequence.

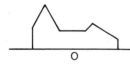

11.   Show the repetition of the given configuration by augmentation (duration).

(continued)

12. Show the repetition of the given configuration by diminution (duration).

_____   _____

13. Show the repetition of the given configuration by vertical expansion.

_____   _____

14. Draw a procession of visually related events based on a configuration of your own choice. First show your original configuration and then show the derived segments. Keep in mind that configurations and segments do not change in retrograde if they are **palindromic**, that is, if they have the same shape in retrograde as they do forward. (The word "madam" is a palindrome.) In your procession of events, use most of the means you know for repetition of both configuration and segments. (Refer to Example 4.13.)

Original configuration (O): _____

Derived segments (S): _____

Procession of events:

_____

_____

15.   Using the given music configuration, write the three basic, derived forms. (Refer to Example 4.4.)

O

I

R

RI

FORM FOR THE PERFORMER

The importance of form for the performer lies chiefly in the obligation to understand the structure of the composition. True artistic performance that faithfully communicates the composer's intent is dependent on careful study and **analysis** of the music, including its formal structure. The performer's obligation extends on the one hand to the listener, who is in need of a well-prepared performance to understand the music, and on the other hand, to the composer, whose music should receive a sensitive and careful presentation.

In analyzing the structure, a performer should be able to identify the means that the composer has used to cultivate each musical idea. The performer might ask such questions as the following.

1. Which musical gestures are important for listeners to hear clearly?

2. What is the important melodic material and how can it be projected?

3. How will each restatement be handled?

4. How can obscured restatements be emphasized?

5. What statements of contrast need emphasis or deemphasis?

6. What special interpretive clues are contained in the manner used to develop each musical idea?

7. What types of phrasing and articulation will most clearly aid the listener in grasping important musical ideas?

8. What is the accompanying material and how can it be kept from dominating more important melodic material?

9. What role will dynamic levels play in balancing unity versus variety?

10. What special performance techniques are needed?

11. What can be done to relate the smaller ideas to the larger sections of the work?

12. How can the overall symmetry and balance be projected to the listener?

13. Are there basic style considerations or traditions associated with the composition which should be in evidence?

The performer's work is never finished. Whether the music is designed for solo performance, small ensemble, or large, the obligation to be aware of the content and organization in various compositions is always present. Completely new views on interpretation can emerge as technique matures and musical understanding develops. Interpretation is also improved by a study of **performance practices** of the past. Not only does this illuminate music from earlier periods of time, but it also provides clearer perspectives on contemporary compositions in all styles. Hence the importance of the notion of the performer-scholar. No detail within the score can be overlooked if a truly honest performance—a performance that best represents the composer's wishes—is to be given. All of this is doubly important for conductors, whose task is to control the efforts of many in order to achieve excellence in performance.

STAFF FOR SKETCHING

CHECK YOUR UNDERSTANDING

Chapter 4, No. 2

1. Supply your own list of items that are important to the performer in giving a faithful and sensitive performance.

_____

_____

_____

_____

_____

_____

_____

_____

_____

_____

_____

2. Explain the difference in performing ostinatos as contrasted with melodic configurations.

_____

_____

_____

_____

_____

STAFF FOR SKETCHING

FORM FOR THE LISTENER

For the listener, the apprehension of form is the peak experience. Of all the parameters of music, form gives the listener the greatest insight into the **aesthetic essence** of music. Unfortunately, the process of apprehending form is a difficult one. Simply stated, it requires a well-developed **musical memory** in order that all aspects of the musical event can be placed into the continuum of sound ordered by the composer. A specific event cannot be reperceived at will; it must be recalled. This is a problem unique to perception in the temporal arts. The graphic arts allow the perceiver to gaze continually at an art object and to organize, classify, and reperceive as often as necessary in order to apprehend more fully the **whole** of the art work. Music listeners, like people watching a movie or a play, or listening to the reading of poetry, are forced by the time variable to perceive, classify, and store the various sound stimuli if, upon completion of the work, they are to grasp the significance of the whole.

Along with the storage and recall processes in listening, one should quickly add the element of expectancy. On the basis of past perceptions during a musical event, listeners are prone to anticipate things to come. Not that their expectations will always be fully rewarded. Actually, the listener would not be happy with a composition in which each event could be predicted, but expectations persist. The listener's approach to the music is based primarily upon skill acquired over a long period of time, on **aural imagery**, and on past musical and cultural experience. One cannot gain a sufficient level of aural sensitivity without long periods of practice and a comprehensive exposure to all kinds of music. It is this type of experience that is necessary if the listener is to enjoy the full impact of the essence of a composition.

STAFF FOR SKETCHING

CHECK YOUR UNDERSTANDING

Chapter 4, No. 3

1. Supply your own list of items that are of concern to listeners in their effort to grasp the rapid procession of events in a composition and to organize them into a comprehensible whole.

_____

_____

_____

_____

_____

_____

_____

_____

_____

_____

_____

_____

_____

2. How would you, as a listener, react to a procession of events in music that was similar to the following visual representation?

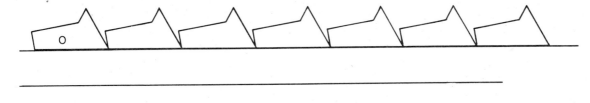

_____

_____

3. How would you, as a listener, react to a procession of events in music that was similar to the following visual representation?

_____

_____

4.   Keeping in mind your answers to Questions 2 and 3, what would be your preference in the way an initial gesture would be treated in the procession of events?

_____

_____

_____

_____

_____

_____

5.   Among the following, underscore only those terms or symbols that refer to
form.

unity   sharp   variety   measure bar   restatement   balance
circle of fifths   binary   scale   musical gesture   mode
design   configuration   submediant   mediant   repetition
retrograde inversion   original   vibration   inversion   segment
retrograde   unison   compound interval   tonal inversion
real inversion   augmentation   sequence   enharmonic
diminution   contraction   ostinato   equal temperament
vertical expansion   interpolation   diatonic   deletion
palindrome

(Be sure you can define all of the above.)

Activities for Developing Music Literacy

AURAL AND KEYBOARD DRILL

1.   Write, read, and chant rhythmic configurations containing from five to seven notes, using the syllable "tah." Chant the same configurations in retrograde, augmentation, and diminution.

Models

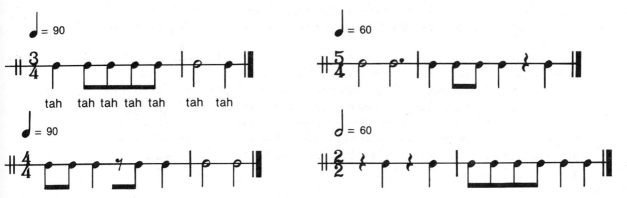

Invent your own configurations and continue practicing the activity.

2.   Write selected diatonic intervals on the staff. Write the original, retrograde, inversion, and retrograde inversion. Sing on the neutral syllable "lah."

Models

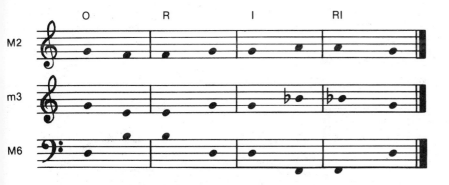

3.   Repeat Drill 2, but notate only the original.

4.   Write a three-note pitch configuration based on a Type 1 tetrachord.* Give each note the duration of one pulse. Write the original and the basic derived forms. Sing.

---

*   The Type 1 tetrachord inverts to a Type 3. Similarly, a Type 3 tetrachord inverts to a Type 1. Type 2 and Type 4 tetrachords do not change types when inverted.

Model

5.   Repeat Drill 4 but notate only the original configuration.

6.   The instructor dictates a simple melodic configuration based on a Type 1 tetra-chord, giving each tone the duration of one pulse. Write the original configuration and any basic variants: retrograde, inversion (tonal), and retrograde inversion.

7.   Write, read, play, and sing a number of different melodic configurations. Limit these configurations to seven tones based on the diatonic scales. Begin with your telephone number, for example 355-7658. Treat each number as a scale degree and a zero as either a rest or scale step 10. Try applying a number of variants to the configurations as suggested in this chapter. The following model is based on the telephone number given above.

Model

DELETION

8. The instructor dictates a five-tone melodic-rhythmic configuration, then dictates one of the basic variants. Write the original and then name the variant.

Model

Instructor plays and student writes:

Instructor plays and student names variant ("inversion"):

9. The instructor writes configurations of five or six tones on a chalkboard or overhead projector, or duplicates them for each student. He or she then plays the configurations on any instrument, introducing a single error of pitch or rhythm in an otherwise perfect performance. Respond by checking the place where the error occurred.

Models

Written: Performed:

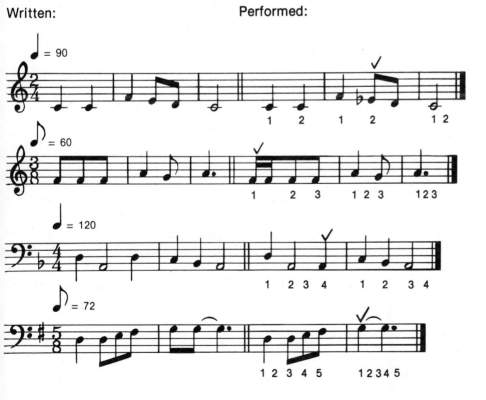

10. The instructor writes configurations of five tones for students. For each configuration, the instructor announces a variant, then plays the correct or a different variant. Indicate whether or not the variant was correct as announced and, if not, what variant was played.

Models

Written: Performed:

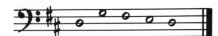   "Retrograde"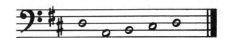

Student judges as incorrect and identifies variant as "inversion."

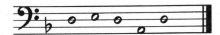   "Inversion"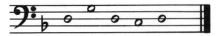

Student judges as incorrect and identifies variant as "retrograde inversion."

Student judges as incorrect and identifies variant as "augmentation."

ANALYTICAL LISTENING

The most effective use of these suggestions would include score study, playing when possible, and repeated listening.

1. Bach, *Well Tempered Clavier*, Vol. I, No. 8, "Fugue in E minor." Performed by Wanda Landowski, RCA Victor Records LM 6801.

   Augmented entrance of **fugue subject** in measure 77.

2. Bach, *Well Tempered Clavier*, Vol. I, No. 6, "Fugue in D minor." Performed by Wanda Landowski, RCA Victor Records LM 6801.

   Inverted entrance of fugue subject in measure 14.

3. Bartók, *Music for String Instruments, Percussion, and Celesta*. Performed by the BBC Symphony Orchestra conducted by Pierre Boulez, Columbia Records MS 7206.

   Inverted form of fugue subject, Movement I, measure 57.

4. Dvořák, *Symphony No. 9* ("The New World"). Performed by The New York Philharmonic Orchestra conducted by Leonard Bernstein, Columbia Records MS 6393.

   Diminution in development section of Movement I, measure 199.

5. Gould, *American Salute*. Performed by The Philadelphia Orchestra conducted by Eugene Ormandy, Columbia Records MS 7289.

   Augmentation of Theme I on third statement.

6. Herman, "Mame," from *Mame*. Performed by the original cast, Columbia Records KOS 3000.

   Sequential development of configuration.

7. Lawrence and Gross, "Tenderly," from *Essential*. Performed by Art Tatum, Verve Records SC 8433.

   Sequential development of configuration.

8. Lai, "Theme from Love Story," from *This is Mancini*, Vol. 2. Performed by Henry Mancini, RCA Victor Records 6053.

   Sequential development of configuration.

9. Willson, *The Music Man*. Performed by the original cast, Capitol Records SW 990.

   Compare the melody (ignoring rhythm) of "Goodnight, My Someone" with that of "Seventy-Six Trombones."

10. Hamilton and Lewis, "How High The Moon," from *Best of Ella*. Performed by Ella Fitzgerald, MCA Records 2-4047.

    Sequential development of configuration.

IMPROVISATION

1. Improvise a rhythmic configuration. Develop it into an extended music event by following the given format for variants:

```
                                A
   O      O      R      O      or      O
                                D
```

   Use neutral syllables, body sounds, or vocal sounds for performing.

2. Improvise a melodic-rhythmic configuration based on a Type 2 tetrachord. By applying a variety of variants, develop an extended composition. It may be helpful to chart the repetitions and variants before beginning the composition. Use any available instrument or voice.

3. Given the ostinato below, improvise a melody based upon the D-major scale. To give the improvisation unity, try to use several variants to develop your original configuration.

CREATIVE WRITING

1. Write a single-voice composition based on a short melodic configuration. Use some transformations to derive variety while maintaining unity. Prepare the score neatly so that it can be performed. Write for any instrument or voice. The composition should be about 30 seconds in length.

2. Choose a four-line poem from any collection of poetry. Set the poem to a melody, being careful to preserve the poem's rhythm. Use the technique of configuration and variants to achieve a unified short composition. Write out carefully with the text, so the class or a small group can perform it.

3. Using the ostinato given below, develop a short composition for two instruments. (One may be the piano.) Again, use the configuration and transformation approach in working out your musical ideas. Prepare a neat, legible score which can easily be performed in class.

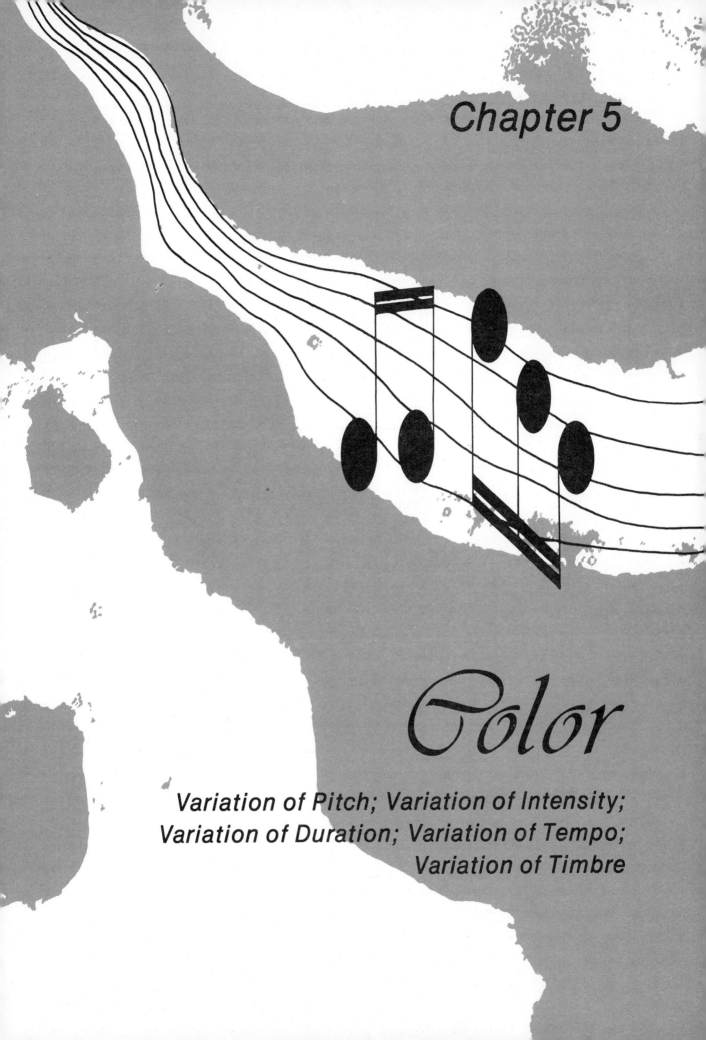

Chapter 5

Color

Variation of Pitch; Variation of Intensity;
Variation of Duration; Variation of Tempo;
Variation of Timbre

The **color** parameter has been defined as variety of effect or expression. Perhaps the most obvious means of achieving variety in music is through the use of different sound sources. This immediately brings to mind different instruments and different voices, hence variety in **timbre**. But variety in musical expression is also achieved by manipulating other variables. In Example 5.1 these variables are listed along with the way expression through that variable is achieved.

Example 5.1
The Color Parameter

VARIABLE	VARIATION CAUSED BY
Pitch	1. Nonvibrato—steady pitch 2. **Vibrato**—fluctuating pitch 3. Bending pitch—slow pitch alteration
Intensity	1. Steady level of tone volume 2. Changing levels of tone volume
Duration	1. Alteration of note length 2. **Articulation** in note connection
Tempo	1. Static tempo 2. Shifting tempo
Timbre	1. Basic instruments and voices of Western and non-Western origins 2. Special performance practices

This chapter will present basic expression techniques available to performers. These include manipulations of pitch, intensity, duration, tempo, and timbre. There will be no attempt to present various practices appropriate to certain instruments and voices. Only the most common variations of each color dimension will be presented, defined, and exemplified.

VARIATION OF PITCH

Current musical performance practices are based on a tuning system known as equal temperament. As you will recall from Chapter 2, in this system the octave is divided into twelve different and equally spaced pitches. Generally speaking, performers on all instruments and singers produce tones which are recognized as being "in tune" with an ideal, abstract pitch based upon this equal-tempered tuning system.

Playing or singing in tune is, or course, necessary for an accurate production of written music, since the composer has conceived the music within the accepted tuning system. Conductors and performers therefore undergo extensive ear training to develop the acute aural sensitivity required for producing pitches that are in tune with one another. Performers, whether in groups or as soloists, must think each pitch carefully before producing it to maintain proper in-tuneness (**intonation**) both melodically and harmonically. Deliberate deviations from the in-tune pitch may, however, be employed when a special effect is desired, this being a manipulation of the color parameter.

The most common pitch variation is that of **vibrato**. Vibrato is a deliberate pitch fluctuation used to color the tone quality of an instrument or voice. The process of vibrato produces a slight, almost imperceptible pitch fluctuation, usually both above and below the actual in-tune pitch. Musicians refer to the center of the pitch as being in tune. The addition of vibrato causes a somewhat even variation above and below the pitch center. Ideally, vibrato is thought to have equal out-of-tuneness either side of the pitch.

Example 5.2
Vibrato Variance

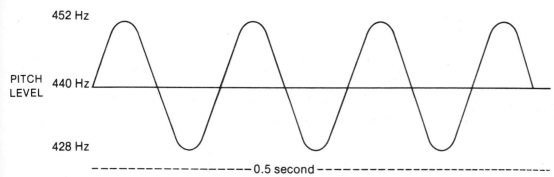

In vibrato, both the speed at which fluctuation takes place and variation in intensity are important. While agreement is somewhat difficult to achieve among performers, the usual speed of fluctuation is roughly 5 to 8 times a second. Fluctuations faster or slower than this are used to achieve further expressive effects. The amount of pitch deviation varies depending upon the basic pitch being played.

Most instruments are capable of producing vibrato. The stringed instruments are rarely played without vibrato, whereas some of the woodwinds seldom use vibrato to color the tone. Vibrato is also used by singers to color tones, but singers disagree over the use of vibrato, as it sometimes causes vocal problems in later years.

The use of vibrato or nonvibrato in performance has varied through the years. What may be the standard now could well be the exception twenty years from now. Particularly with the advent of electronically amplified tones, instruments of all types have the capability of producing vibrato. Since some individual performance specialists advocate the use of vibrato and others do not, there is no absolute standard that can be reported. Composers can, however, request or deter vibrato from performers as needed for expressive purposes. They do this by simply writing *vibrato* or *vib.*, *no vibrato* or *no vib*. Many 20th century composers have chosen to be more precise than this, using symbols to indicate the use of nonvibrato (——————), the speed of

vibrato

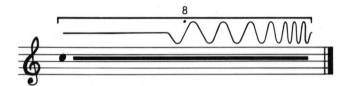

slow   fast

and the amount of pitch fluctuation

narrow   wide

Example 5.3 illustrates how this notation is sometimes used in new music. The example also shows notation for nonmeasured music. The extension line after the note head signifies pitch duration for the number of seconds indicated by the sign ⌐——8——⌐.

Example 5.3
Vibrato in New Music

Two other pitch inflection procedures not common to art music but found occasionally in jazz writing are the **bend** and the **fall off**, or **spill**. The bend calls for a deliberate pitch dip and return to original pitch. The indication for this type of expressive event is usually as follows.

BEND

ρ   or   ρ

In the case of the fall-off or spill, the composer desires a descent in pitch, usually following a climax. This is indicated as follows.

LONG FALL-OFF   SHORT FALL-OFF

CHECK YOUR UNDERSTANDING

Chapter 5, No. 1

1. Define the term color as it relates to music. _____
   _____
   _____

2. What variables can be manipulated by composers and performers to produce
   changes in color?_____
   _____
   _____

3. Describe the equal temperament tuning system. _____
   _____
   _____
   _____

4. Define vibrato. _____
   _____
   _____
   _____

5. Among the following, underscore only those terms or symbols that refer to
   color.

   timbre   configuration   expansion   vibrato   segment   bend
   beam   fall off   harmonics   nonvibrato   unit   pitch
   fluctuation

   (Be sure you can define all of the above.)

STAFF FOR SKETCHING

VARIATION OF INTENSITY

Intensity refers to the relative loudness or softness of tones. As such it constitutes an important variable in the color parameter for composers and ultimately for performers and conductors. It is necessary to think of the intensity variable from two points of view: (1) steady levels of tone volume, and (2) changing levels of tone volume. Both of these factors have a significant effect on color.

The range of **dynamics**, or intensity levels, indicated in Example 5.4 includes only the most common terms and symbols found in music. The meanings of the various designations are only relative, for there is no absolute or exact **decibel** level that serves as a reference point. Decisions regarding what is "soft" or what is "very, very loud" are therefore left to the discretion of the conductor or performer. Final decisions are affected by the number of performers, availability of amplification, acoustics of the place of performance, strengths and weaknesses of various players, and so forth.

Example 5.4
Steady Intensity Level Indications*

ENGLISH	ITALIAN TERM	ABBREVIATION
As soft as possible	*pianississimo*	*ppp*
Very soft	*pianissimo*	*pp*
Soft	*piano*	*p*
Medium soft	*mezzo piano*	*mp*
Medium loud	*mezzo forte*	*mf*
Loud	*forte*	*f*
Very loud	*fortissimo*	*ff*
As loud as possible	*fortississimo*	*fff*

Dynamic level indicators in music are placed both above and below notes. In instrumental music, it is traditional to place intensity level abbreviations below the note where the prescribed dynamic is to begin. But in vocal music, because of the presence of text, abbreviations for dynamic levels are placed above the note where the level is to begin.

One of the most striking means of obtaining intensity level change is by the use of **dynamic accent** signs. Of these, the two most frequently used are ♪ and ♪ . Both are percussive in nature. Of the two, the ∧ is used when stronger accent is desired at a higher dynamic level. Both of these accent types are placed at the note head, but when the stem is up, the second accent sign (∧) is inverted and placed below the note head (♪).

---

* No attempt will be made to list intensity indications in all languages.
Contemporary composers often use more extreme dynamic levels (*ppppp*—*fffff*).
Composers often choose to use the term *sempre*, or "always," with dynamic level indications when the level is to remain constant for a long time.

Example 5.5
Placement of Dynamic Symbols

a) Henry Fillmore, *His Honor*

b) Robert A. Harris, *Glory to God*

---

*   The small 8 under the treble clef sign indicates performance an octave lower than written.

The use of dynamic or intensity level indicators is a much more common practice today than throughout earlier periods of Western music. Composers are careful to indicate exact levels as best they can and performers must be careful to follow the composer's instructions. Frequently, music from other cultures or earlier Western music contains dynamic indications added by editors or musicologists. While one could quarrel with their designations on occasion, students are advised to follow their markings as closely as possible. The research and scholarly training of these people has, in all probability, brought about the most appropriate indications.

Another important way in which intensity level is manipulated is through the use of changing dynamics. The most common terms and symbols that are used to designate changing intensity are contained in Example 5.6.

Example 5.6
Changing Intensity Level Indications*

ENGLISH	ITALIAN TERM	ABBREVIATION	SYMBOL
Gradually louder	*crescendo*	*cresc.*	
Gradually softer	*diminuendo* or *decrescendo*	*dim.* *decresc.*	

Although terms from other languages are not included here, it is important for performers and conductors to be familiar with all words and symbols that relate to intensity variation. Performers must develop the skill to produce gradual increases and decreases in intensity to portray faithfully the composers' intent.

Two qualifying terms are commonly used to identify the speed at which intensity levels are to increase or decrease:

1. **Subito** means "suddenly"; hence *subito p* would mean suddenly soft.
2. **Poco a poco** means "little by little"; hence *cresc. poco a poco* would mean to grow in intensity little by little.

Similarly, the *crescendo* mark is used to indicate the speed of *crescendo* and *diminuendo* as follows.

p ——————————————————— *f*   *f* ——▷ *p*
           (slowly louder)   (quickly softer)

---

*   For other terms related to intensity variation, the interested student may consult any of several music dictionaries, which give a complete listing of these kinds of terms in all languages. An excellent standard reference is Willi Apel, *Harvard Dictionary of Music* (Cambridge, Mass.: Harvard University Press, 1965).

Dynamic levels (p, mf, f) should always be included with *crescendo/diminuendo* marks. The use of these marks is illustrated in Example 5.7.

Example 5.7
The Crescendo and Diminuendo Marks

Randall Thompson, "The Lord is My Shepherd"

CHECK YOUR UNDERSTANDING

Chapter 5, No. 2

1. Define intensity. _____

_____

2. What two dimensions of intensity can be manipulated by music creators? ____

_____

_____

3. Fill in the following blanks.

   a) To indicate that something is to be performed very softly the composer uses

   _____

   b) To indicate that something is to gain in intensity the composer uses

   _____

   c) _____ means to play gradually softer.

   d) _____ means to play at a loud level.

   e) Either _____ or _____ indicates a medium intensity.

4. Using abbreviations, indicate the various stages in the soft-to-loud intensity continuum below.

   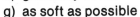

   Soft   Loud

5. Place symbols for the suggested intensity variations in the folk song "Greensleeves" at the points indicated.

   a) soft   b) gradually louder   c) loud
   d) gradually softer   e) soft   f) gradually softer
   g) as soft as possible

191

6.   Among the following, underscore only those terms or symbols that refer to *intensity*.

decibel   retrograde   dynamic level   fast   *mezzo piano*   *forte*
crescendo   timbre   *dim.*   *mf*   *pp*   parameter   ═══════◁
subito p   palindrome   *poco a poco cresc.*   intonation

(Be sure you can define all of the above.)

VARIATION OF DURATION

Another way of achieving variation in color is by modifying duration. This is done by altering note lengths with symbols and indicating the specific manner in which groups of notes are to be articulated. The term **articulation** refers to the ways tones are attacked, sustained, released, and connected.

Aside from the traditional dotted, tied, and undotted notes, composers have chosen to use a wide variety of terms and symbols to alter duration of sound. The problem of *exact* note values has never been entirely resolved. A quarter note which is to receive a beat is sometimes held full value and sometimes not. But regardless of the articulation used (see Example 5.8), all quarter-note unit beats are conceived in the same basic pulse; that is, ♩ is actually performed approximately as ♪ ╮ with the pulse rate unchanged. The difference between ♩ and ♩̇ is only in the duration of the tones (after their identical initial onset) and the alteration that is indicated occurs *within the framework of one pulse*. The *exact* length is determined by performers and depends on a host of other variables in the music.

Performers have developed certain conventions in relation to duration that characterize or provide the basic style for different kinds of music. Within the last two centuries composers have become particularly aware of duration problems and want their music to be interpreted accurately. Such concern has brought about a whole set of symbols and terms to assist the performer. The most common interpretive marks and symbols for duration alteration are contained in Example 5.8.

Example 5.8
Duration Alteration Symbols

SYMBOL	ENGLISH TERM	ITALIAN TERM
♩	Very short	*staccatissimo*
♩	Short	*staccato*
♩	Long but disconnected	*tenuto*
	Longer but disconnected	*portato*
	Still longer, but slightly disconnected	*legato*
	Slurred, connected, not broken	*legatura*
𝄐	Held for extra duration	*fermata*

These symbols have special significance for certain instruments. For example, in string instrument performance they may indicate bow strokes. The word **simile** or **sim**. ("in a similar way") indicates the continued use of a bowing or articulation previously specified.

The following pairs of quarter notes are arranged from the shortest to the longest values according to the symbols outlined in Example 5.8. The unaltered quarter note is also included in this continuum.

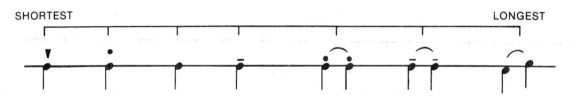

Naturally, conductors and performers have to be extremely familiar with and able to execute all of these note lengths. Again, the purpose is to recreate faithfully what the composer has indicated. Therefore the composer must indicate very carefully all variations in duration that are necessary to communicate the musical ideas.

Once a clear understanding of all the variations in duration is gained, the performer must put these into practice by playing long series of notes with special attention to the ways they are articulated. All combinations of durational symbols can be found in music. Perhaps the two most common are the slur and the staccato. Example 5.9 shows staccato and slur in instrumental music.

Example 5.9
Mozart, *Concerto No. 4 in E Major for Horn* (K. 495), Movement III, Theme 1

Combinations such as these are common and produce significant expressive differences in music. Traditions and styles vary greatly from instrument to instrument and cannot be fully treated in this chapter. Students are charged with the responsibility for grasping traditional practices for their instrument or voice.

Similar articulation indications are found in choral and solo vocal music. It is common to find the vowel sound extended over more than one pitch, thus producing a slur. A shortened durational value is often found in order to increase spacing between notes. Both of these practices are shown in Example 5.10.

Example 5.10
Diemer, "Sing O Heavens," SATB

STAFF FOR SKETCHING

CHECK YOUR UNDERSTANDING

Chapter 5, No. 3

1. Explain how duration pertains to color. _____
    _____
    _____

2. Identify the chief color variables which can be classified as durational.

    _____ _____ and _____ _____

3. Define the following terms.

    a) *legato* _____

    b) *portato* _____

    c) *staccato* _____

    d) *fermata* _____

    e) *tenuto* _____

4. Using the duration-alteration symbols, fill in the following blanks with quarter notes as indicated.

    a) ♩ is longer than _____

    b) ♩ ♩ is longer than _____

    c) ♩ ♩ is longer than _____

    d) ♩ ♩ is longer than _____

5. Among the following, underscore only those terms or symbols that refer to *duration alteration*.

    staccato   *mf*   poco a poco dim.   tenuto   portato   ♩   ♪   ♩

    ♩ ♩   slur   ♩   transposition   interpolation

    articulation

    (Be sure you can define all of the above.)

STAFF FOR SKETCHING

VARIATION OF TEMPO

One of the greatest expressive tools available to the performer is tempo variation. Today the use of tempo fluctuation for expressive purposes has reached a high level of artistic development, and all performers need to possess a keen sense of tempo. This was not always the case, for performers did not exploit the use of tempo fluctuation until about the 19th century in Western music history. Prior to that time tempo was relatively stable and rarely did performers change musical pace to express more poignantly a composer's idea.

Composers indicate tempo in two ways. In the first method, a tempo term is used that enjoys a somewhat universal meaning. In the second method, the composer indicates tempo by indentifying the unit and the number of units per minute ($\quarternote$ = 96). This latter practice enables the composer and the performer to determine the tempo with a metronome, as explained in Chapter 1. At times composers indicate a range of tempo, rather than one single speed ($\quarternote$ = 84 - 92). The most common tempo terms are given with Italian equivalents in Example 5.11. The approximate speeds in beats per minute are shown in relation to the continuum from very slow (40) to very fast (240). There has been too much variation in identifying terms with metronomic indications to be more specific.

Example 5.11
Common Tempo Terms

ENGLISH	ITALIAN	BEATS PER MINUTE CONTINUUM
Very slow	**Largo**	40
Slow	**Lento**	
Easy	**Adagio**	60
Walking pace	**Andante**	
Moderately	**Moderato**	
Quick	**Allegro**	120
Fast	**Presto**	
Very fast	**Prestissimo**	240

Several other terms must be understood to interpret correctly the tempo directions given by most composers. These terms include:

meno mosso—less motion

piu mosso—more motion

tempo giusto—strict tempo

tempo primo (Tempo I)—original tempo

A tempo indication that requires particularly sensitive treatment by the performer is the term **rubato**, which literally means "to rob." In effect the performer decreases and increases pulse speed in a balanced manner in order to express the music. But these differences are slight. It is crucial to understand that rubato involves both give *and* take. The performer needs to have a good sense of the whole composition in order to balance any increases in pulse speed with subsequent decreases. Either should offset the other. *Rubato is often overused*.

Composers also indicate tempo fluctuation in their music by a group of terms which should become familiar to all musicians. Some of the more important terms are listed with Italian equivalents in Example 5.12. These terms are traditionally placed below the notes in instrumental music at the point where the change is to begin. In vocal music these terms are placed above the staff.

Example 5.12
Tempo Modification Terms

ENGLISH	ITALIAN	ABBREVIATION
Gradually faster	**accelerando** or **stringendo**	*accel.* *string.*
Gradually slower	**rallentando** or **ritardando**	*rall.* *rit.* or *ritard.*

To indicate return to the previous tempo after one of these modification, composers use the term *a tempo*.

VARIATION OF TIMBRE

Chapter 4 illustrated the growth of a musical configuration by means of a visual configuration. The following visual configuration shows the impact color has on the restatement-contrast relationship. In terms of music, the various internal designs of the visual configuration represent different tone qualities, and thus constitute another way of achieving variety while at the same time retaining unity.

Example 5.13
The Variation of a Visual Configuration Through Color Change

A part of Example 5.13 might be realized musically as in Example 5.14. Here variety is achieved only by timbre change.

Example 5.14
The Variation of a Musical Configuration Through Timbre Change

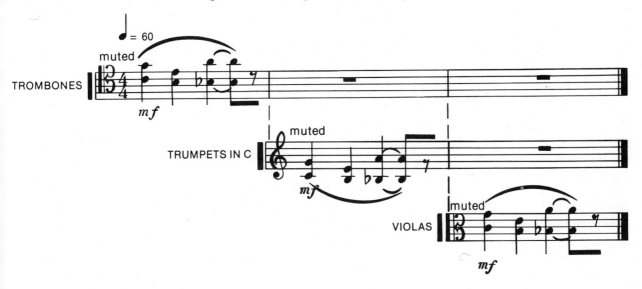

Example 5.14 incorporates several fundamental concepts in the ordering of music parameters. The books that follow in this series will extend your understanding of parameters and the way composers control them to produce the total musical effect.

STAFF FOR SKETCHING

_____

(Name)

CHECK YOUR UNDERSTANDING

Chapter 5, No. 4

1. Define the following terms.

    a) *rubato*: _____

    _____

    b) *presto*: _____

    c) *adagio*: _____

    d) *andante*: _____

    e) *lento*: _____

2. Explain the use of *rubato* as it relates to the overall time of performance for a composition.

    _____

    _____

    _____

    _____

3. Describe in your own words the problem relating to tempo indications by term rather than by the tempo-unit method.

    _____

    _____

    _____

    _____

4. Arrange the following terms in order from slowest to fastest.

    allegro   lento   largo   andante   presto   adagio

    a)_____ b)_____ c)_____

    d)_____ e)_____ f)_____

5. Vary the music configuration below (portion in brackets) by the use of **intensity variation** only. Use the abbreviations given in this chapter.

6.   Vary the music configuration below by the use of **duration alteration** symbols. These symbols may be combined with intensity variation.

7.   Vary the music configuration below by the use of **tempo variation**. These symbols may be combined with intensity and duration alteration.

8.   Among the following, underscore only those terms or symbols that refer to *variation of tempo* or *timbre change*.

meno mosso   *cresc.*   *tempo primo*   *dim.*   *rubato*   *accel.*
segment   *ritard.*   *stringendo*   *forte*   *rall.*   muted
sempre ƒ

(Be sure you can define all of the above.)

Activities for Developing Music Literacy

AURAL AND KEYBOARD DRILL

Many of the activities are of a review nature, stressing the importance of continuing aural drills to form secure aural understanding.

1.   On the chalkboard, the instructor writes a Type 1 tetrachord beginning on any pitch. After playing the first pitch, he or she points to various notes in the tetrachord. Respond by singing pitches for the indicated notes. Sing at various intensity levels.

2.   After playing the starting tone for a Type 1 tetrachord, the instructor plays four-note groups based on the tetrachord. Write notes on the staff to correspond to the tones played. Check for accuracy. Be sure to use various registers of the piano to expand perception skills.

3.   The instructor dictates short configurations (four or five tones) based on various tetrachord types, and using pulses, divisions, ties between pulses, and rests. Write notes on the staff to correspond. Measure signatures may be included.

Model

Instructor plays and student writes:

4.   Given the first tone on an instrument, sing or play major scales. If singing, use numbers, letters, and neutral syllables. Apply several articulation patterns if playing on an instrument. Use different neutral syllables or slurred tones if singing.

Model

5.   Play and sing all intervals that can be derived from the major and minor scales. Refer to Aural and Keyboard Drill 21, Chapter 3.

Model

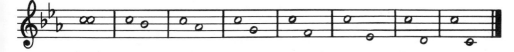

(A similar model for the major scale can be found on page 146.)

6.   Write a five-tone pitch configuration based on any type of tetrachord. Give each tone the duration of a pulse. After successfully singing the original configuration, sing it in at least one variant.

Model

7.   Write, read, and sing melodic configurations with and without rhythmic patterns. Limit these configurations to seven tones based on diatonic scales. Apply at least one transformation to these longer configurations.

8.   Write from dictation a seven-tone configuration performed by voice or instrument. Clearly communicate dynamic levels and changing dynamics.

Model

9.   Write from dictation a short configuration which uses a variety of kinds of articulation. Limit it to five tones and Type 1 or Type 2 tetrachords.

10.   Sing various melodic passages, adding color through dynamics and articulation. Alter both dynamics and articulation to create differences in style. See Appendix 3 for further materials.

Model
Scarlatti, *Sonata in C* (Longo 205)

11. Write from dictation several melodic/rhythmic configurations that use a variety of color variants: (a) dynamics, (b) articulation, (c) tempo changes. When the configurations are repeated with alterations of color, indicate which color element(s) changed on the second playing.

Model
"Black is the Color of My True Love's Hair" (Folk)

Instructor plays and student writes:

Instructor plays:

Student responds: Dynamics and articulation.

12. Play short melodies at the piano. Use different articulation patterns, dynamics, and tempos to create different interpretations.

Model
"Copper Kettle" (American Folk)

13. Study music you are performing, noting all color indications. Be sure to follow these indications carefully when performing, as they are crucial to an accurate representation of the music.

14. Select solo material you are playing and experiment with a variety of color effects: vibrato, dynamics, tempo, and articulation. Try to understand the composers' and/or editors' reasons for suggesting different color variations.

ANALYTICAL LISTENING

Careful study of the score will enhance your listening and produce greater aural perception.

1. American Folk, "Black is the Color of My True Love's Hair," in *The Hi-Lo's Happen To Folk Songs*. Performed by the Hi-Lo's, Reprise Records R 6034.

   Tempo *rubato* throughout and exceptional variations in dynamics.

2. Comenor, "Lovin' Stew." Performed by The Fifth Dimension, Soul City Records 779.

   Articulation in vocal chorus as opposed to instrumental articulations. Tempo variation.

3. Dixon, "You Shook Me," on *Pop Origins*. Performed by Muddy Waters, Chess Records LP 1544.

   Articulations in vocal solo and background. Slowly growing dynamic level and fadeout.

4. Gershwin, "Summertime," from *Smithsonian Collection of Classic Jazz*. Performed by Miles Davis with the Gil Evans Orchestra, Washington, D.C.: Smithsonian Institution, 1973.

   Articulation throughout and occasional use of pitch fluctuation for effect.

5. Harrison, "Something." Performed by The Beatles, Apple Records 2654.

   Dynamics throughout, tempo variations and variations in pitch during vocal chorus.

6. Joplin, "Solace," from *The Sting*. Performed by Marvin Hamlish, MCA Records 390.

   Extensive use of slurring, connected articulations particularly in instruments. Compare to the instrumental version of "The Entertainer," next band on album.

7. Mozart, *Overture to The Marriage of Figaro*. Performed by the Cleveland Orchestra conducted by George Szell, Columbia Records ML 6258.

   Dynamics, articulation between winds and strings at the beginning.

8. Ravel, "Pavane Pour Une Infante Défunte," on *The Art of Julian Bream*. Performed by Julian Bream, RCA Victor LM 2448.

   Tempo *rubato* throughout.

9. Respighi, "The Pine of Villa Borghese," from *The Pines of Rome*. Performed by the Philadelphia Orchestra conducted by Eugene Ormandy, Columbia Records M 30829.

   Dynamic levels at the beginning. Also compare dynamic level with the opening of "The Pines Near a Catacomb," band 2 of the album.

10. Rogers, "Dance of Mourning," from *Three Japanese Dances*. Performed by the Eastman Wind Ensemble conducted by Frederick Fennell, Mercury Records MG 50173.

    Vibrato in solo soprano voice; dynamics and changing dynamics during and after vocal solo.

IMPROVISATION

1. Use any of the creative writing assignments from previous chapters to explore the effect of tempo and dynamic differences. Perform several of these assignments with improvised differences in dynamics and static or changing tempo.

2. As in Chapter 1, create a rhythmic canon of 12 pulses. Divide the group or class into three parts and perform. Discuss the need for dynamic contrasts in order to produce the greatest musical effect.

3. Improvise at the piano or on instruments. Decide on a basic configuration and several variants. Apply various color factors such as different kinds of articulation, changing dynamics, and rubato.

4. Improvise a part above an ostinato based on a selected diatonic scale. Use various color factors to enrich the performance. Be sensitive to other players and complement their articulation and dynamic levels where appropriate. If there are two players, assign one per part. If there are three or more players, assign one to the ostinato and have others improvise their own parts.

Model
(In D Phrygian)

CREATIVE WRITING

1. Prepare a 30- to 60-second composition for two instruments. One instrument will produce an ostinato while the other explores a configuration, segments, and several variants. Be sure to repeat the configuration in recognizable form several times to maintain unity. Use various tempos, dynamic levels, and dynamic shadings. Include varied articulation patterns to fit the instruments, and take care to mark everything exactly as you wish it to be played.

2. Choose a poem from any source and set it for two voices. One part should function like an ostinato or rhythmic chant. The other voice should follow the text. Include repetitions of parts of the text, various kinds of articulation for voice (slurring of vowels, staccato, or wider-spaced sounds), and very accurate dynamics. Prepare the score carefully for performance in class.

Model
Edgar A. Poe, "El Dorado"

Gaily bedight, a gallant knight,
       in sunshine and in shadow,
traveled long, singing a song
       in search of El Dorado.

    Ostinato could be: traveled long, singing a song
                          traveled long, singing a song

Appendixes

Glossary/Index; Triad Nomenclature;
Source Material for Developing Music Literacy;
Answers to CYU's

Appendix 1: Glossary/Index

Note: The definitions provided here are not intended to be all-inclusive, but can aid the student in gaining initial understanding. When a music term is first mentioned in the text, it is placed in boldface type; however, that passage may not contain the most complete discussion.

accelerando (*accel.*)	A gradual increase in tempo.	200
accent	The application of emphasis to a particular musical sound.	5, 14, 187
accidental	See *alteration signs*.	
acoustics	The science of sound.	2*n*
adagio	A slow tempo—slower than *andante* but faster than *lento* or *largo*. See also *tempo, pace*.	199
Aeolian mode	A diatonic scale formed from the combination of a Type 2 plus a Type 3 tetrachord joined by a whole step, for example, white keys A to A.	104, 115
aesthetic essence	The expressive content of a music composition.	171
allegro	A moderately fast tempo—slower than *presto* but faster than *moderato*. See also *tempo, pace*.	199
alteration signs ♯ ♭ × ♭♭ ♮	Symbols placed before notes to alter the pitch of a musical tone. See also *sharp, flat, double sharp, double flat, natural*.	57, 58, 135*ff*
alto clef	A symbol designating a note on the middle line of the five-line staff as C4, or middle C. See also *bass clef, neutral clef, tenor clef, treble clef*.	66, 67, 70
amplitude	The vertical distance between the extreme points of a sound wave. Amplitude produces intensity.	2
analysis	A careful examination of the parameters of music.	167
andante	A moderate tempo—slower than *allegro* but faster than *adagio*. See also *tempo, pace*.	199
arpeggiated	Term indicating that chord tones are sounded in succession rather than simultaneously.	89
articulation	The manner in which tones are attacked, sustained, released, and connected in performance.	10, 182
ascending	A term used to describe scales or melodies that rise in pitch.	65*n*
a tempo	At the original tempo.	200
augmentation	The technique or varying a configuration or segment by increasing the duration of notes.	159
aural imagery	An ability to imagine sound by viewing and studying a musical score.	171
balance	The equilibrium between unity and variety within a musical composition.	154*ff*
barlines	Lines drawn perpendicular to the staff to create measures.	29*ff*
basic scale	A successive set of adjacent tones produced by the seven white keys on the piano.	52, 86, 127

basic triads		The seven triads constructed on the white keys of the piano. See *triads*.	86
bass clef	𝄢	A symbol designating a note on the fourth line of the five-line staff as F3. See also *alto clef, neutral clef, tenor clef, treble clef*.	67*ff*
beams	▬	Lines used to connect the stems of multiple 8th, 16th, and 32nd notes in order to facilitate grouping and music reading.	19*ff*
beat		The basic temporal pulse in a music composition. See also *pulse, unit of beat*.	14*ff*
bend	♪	A dip in pitch of usually less than a half step.	184
binary form		A two-part form.	154
borrowed division		See *irregular division*.	
C clef	𝄡	See *alto clef, tenor clef*.	66*ff*
canon		A polyphonic composition in which a melody, stated in one part, is imitated (followed) for the length of the composition.	50
chord		Three or more tones sounding simultaneously.	9, 85*ff*
chord quality		See *quality of chord*.	
chromatic scale		A series of tones that are produced by consecutively playing all twelve half steps in the octave.	53
circle of fifths		A circular arrangement of tonic notes or scales illustrating their transposition (by perfect fifths) to all twelve key centers.	127*ff*
clef signs		See *alto clef, bass clef, neutral clef, tenor clef, treble clef*.	65*ff*
color		One of the five parameters of music, defined as variety of effect or expression.	9, 10, 181*ff*
compound intervals		Intervals that span more than an octave: 9ths, 10ths, 11ths, etc.	76
conducting patterns		Motions used by conductors to communicate pulse organizations to performers.	35*ff*
configuration (cf)		A small musical germ idea (often an initial gesture) that has natural developmental or formal tendencies.	9, 155*ff*
contraction		The technique of varying a configuration or segment by decreasing the size of melodic intervals.	159, 160
contrast		The use of variety to achieve interest in a composition.	155*ff*
crescendo (*cresc.*)	◁	A term used to indicate a gradual increase in intensity.	189, 190
decibel (db)		A term used to express the intensity of a sound.	3, 4, 187
decrescendo (*decresc.*)	▷	A term used to indicate a gradual decrease in intensity.	189, 190
deletion		The technique of varying a configuration or segment by omitting one or more tones.	160

descending	A term used to describe scales or melodies that fall in pitch.	65n
diatonic intervals	Intervals derived from diatonic scales.	146, 147, 175
diatonic melody	A melody based on a diatonic scale.	106
diatonic scale	A scale of seven tones within an octave comprising some arrangement of five whole steps and two half steps. But see the more complete definition on page 104. See also *scale*.	52, 104ff, 113ff
dictation	The process of converting sounds into notation.	41ff, 145, 146
diminuendo (dim.)	A term used to indicate a gradual decrease in intensity.	189, 190
diminution	The technique of varying a configuration or segment by decreasing the duration of the notes.	159
division	The fractional partitioning of duration. See also *regular division, irregular division*.	21ff
dominant	The fifth tone of a diatonic scale.	106
Dorian mode	A diatonic scale formed from the combination of a Type 2 plus a Type 2 tetrachord joined by a whole step, for example, white keys D to D.	105, 115
dotted note	A note whose duration is extended by the use of a dot. The dot increases the assigned value of the note by one-half.	21ff
double bar	Two adjacent barlines, used to separate or terminate sections of a composition.	30
double flat ♭♭	A symbol that lowers a natural note two half steps or an already flatted note an additional half step.	57
double sharp ✕	A symbol that raises a natural note two half steps or an already sharped note an additional half step.	57
duration	The length of time assigned to notes and rests.	2, 5, 19ff, 182, 193, 194
dynamic accent > ∧ ∨	A symbol signifying greater dynamic level.	105, 187
dynamic level *mf pf*	The intensity of sound specified for a given section of a composition.	10, 187
enharmonic equivalents	Multiple names for a single pitch, as F♯ and G♭ in equal temperament.	57, 58, 128
equal temperament	A system of tuning that divides the octave into twelve different and equally spaced pitches.	52, 182
eurhythmics	A system for developing rhythmic sensitivity through body motion.	44n
expansion	The technique of varying a configuration or segment by increasing the size of the melodic intervals.	159, 160
F clef 𝄢	See *bass clef*.	
fall off	A downward slide in pitch from a given tone.	184

fermata ⌢	A symbol used to extend the duration of a tone beyond its indicated length.	193
15*ma*	A symbol indicating that the notated pitches should be performed two octaves higher or lower than written. See also *8va (ottava)*.	69
flags ⃥⃥	Small curved lines attached to single note stems to indicate duration. An eighth note has one flag, a sixteenth, two, etc.	19
flat ♭	A symbol that alters a natural pitch by lowering it one half step. See also *alteration signs*.	57
form	The organizational structure of music.	9, 153*ff*
forte f	Loud.	187
fortissimo ff	Very loud.	187
fortississimo fff	As loud as possible.	187
frequency	The position of a pitch on the continuum from high to low, according to the number of vibrations per second.	2, 3, 52
fugue	A polyphonic composition based on an initial configuration (subject). See also *subject*.	178
fundamental	The perceived pitch of a tone; the first harmonic.	3, 4, 5
G clef 𝄞	See *treble clef*.	
general intervals	The nonspecific pitch difference between two tones: primes (unisons), seconds, thirds, fourths, fifths, sixths, sevenths, eighths, ninths, etc. See also *specific intervals*.	75, 76
gesture	See *musical gesture*.	
grace note	A very short note whose durational value takes time from an adjacent note.	20
grand staff	A combination of two five-line staffs, usually with a treble clef on the upper staff and a bass clef on the lower staff. Piano music is written on the grand staff.	61, 69, 70
half step	A pitch difference equal to 1/12 of an octave, or the difference between adjacent piano keys.	53
harmonic interval	The vertical alignment and simultaneous sounding of two pitches.	9, 75*ff*, 81*ff*
harmonic minor scale	A nondiatonic scale formed by raising the seventh tone of the Aeolian mode a half step. But see footnote on page 122.	121*ff*
harmonic series	See *harmonics*.	
harmonics	The pitches that occur as a part of a composite tone.	3, 4, 5

harmony	The study of the vertical structure of music and of the horizontal movement of chords.	9, 51*ff*
hertz (Hz)	A unit of measurement for pitch equal to the number of vibrations per second, as A = 440 Hz.	2, 52
homophonic	Musical texture characterized by chordal support of a melodic line. See also *monophonic, polyphonic*.	9*n*
improvisation	The spontaneous expression of musical ideas through performance.	48*ff*
indeterminacy	Music composed through chance procedures or unpredictable in performance, often called "aleatory."	14, 151
intensity	A term used to describe the loudness or softness of tones.	2, 3, 182, 187*ff*
interpolation	The technique of varying a configuration or segment by adding tones.	160
interpretive symbols	Abbreviations and symbols such as p, mf, f, *cresc.*, *dim.*, etc. used to alter music performance.	182*ff*
interval	The distance between two pitches sounded simultaneously or successively. See also *general intervals, specific intervals*.	52, 75*ff*, 81*ff*
interval inversion	See *inversion of intervals*.	
inversion	See *inversion of intervals, melodic inversion, retrograde inversion, real inversion, tonal inversion*.	
inversion of intervals	The process of turning a harmonic interval upside down.	81*ff*
intonation	A term used to describe the performance of a musical tone in relation to a standard of precise pitch: playing or singing in tune.	183
Ionian mode	A diatonic scale formed from the combination of a Type 1 plus a Type 1 tetrachord joined by a whole step, for example, white keys C to C.	105, 106, 114
irregular division	The fractional partitioning of a note using other than regular division, for example,	21*n*

See also *regular division*.

key center	The tonic note of a key, as C in the key of C; or B♭ in the key of B♭.	106, 135*ff*
key signature	A group of sharps or flats at the beginning of a piece of music.	9, 129*n*, 130, 135*ff*
largo	A very slow tempo—slower than *lento*.	199
leading tone	The seventh tone of a diatonic scale (minor second below the tonic).	106, 107, 122
ledger lines	Lines added above or below the staff to accommodate notes above or below the staff.	66*ff*
legato	A term used to indicate that tones are to be fully sustained but slightly disconnected.	193, 194

legatura	A term used to indicate that tones are to be slurred. See *slur*.	193, 194
lento	A slow tempo—slightly faster than *largo* and slower than *adagio*.	199
line	An orderly, horizontal succession of tones.	9, 104, 123
Locrian mode	A diatonic scale formed from the combination of a Type 3 plus a Type 4 tetrachord joined by a half step, for example, white keys B to B.	104, 115
Lydian mode	A diatonic scale formed from the combination of a Type 4 plus a Type 1 tetrachord joined by a half step, for example, white keys F to F.	105, 115
Maelzel	The inventor of the metronome, a device to produce specific speeds of pulse accurately.	15
major mode	A scale or mode whose tonic triad is major.	121
major scale	A diatonic scale formed from the combination of a Type 1 plus a Type 1 tetrachord joined by a whole step, for example, white keys C to C.	105, 106, 121
measure	The space between two consecutive barlines in music notation.	29*ff*
measure signature	A combination of numerals and/or symbols indicating the amount of music notation to be contained in each measure.	30*ff*
mediant	The third tone of a diatonic scale.	106
melodic interval	The pitch difference between two successive tones.	9, 53, 107*n*, 146*ff*
melodic inversion	The technique of varying a configuration or segment by changing an ascending line to a complementary descending line, or vice versa.	157*ff*
melody	An orderly, horizontal succession of tones perceived as the dominating line. See *line*.	9, 103*ff*, 156*ff*
meno mosso	A direction to slacken the pace or tempo; literally, "less motion."	199
meter	The manner in which pulses are grouped.	29*ff*, 37
metronome	A device than produces pulse at a variety of tempos. See also *Maelzel*.	15, 36
mezzo forte mf	Medium loud.	187
mezzo piano mp	Medium soft.	187
minor mode	A scale or mode whose tonic triad is minor.	122
minor scale	A scale whose tonic triad is minor, normally the "harmonic minor" scale or "Aeolian minor."	105, 114, 115, 121*ff*
Mixolydian mode	A diatonic scale formed from the combination of a Type 1 plus a Type 2 tetrachord joined by a whole step, for example, white keys G to G.	105, 114
modal key signatures	See *key signatures*.	
moderato	A tempo indication faster than *andante* but slower than *allegro*.	199

modes	A group of diatonic scales, for example, those formed by starting on each of the white piano keys and ascending an octave, playing each white key consecutively.	104*ff*, 113*ff*
modulate	To change to a new key center.	135
monophonic	Musical texture characterized by a single melodic line without accompaniment. See also *homophonic, polyphonic*.	9*n*
motion	The illusion of sounds moving in time, best exemplified by the conductor's gestures.	35*ff*
musical gesture	A short musical idea that possesses characteristics that make development possible; a configuration.	154
musical memory	An important dimension of musical ability; the ability to retain and recall musical events after occurrence.	171
natural ♮	A symbol that cancels a previous sharp or flat.	57
neutral clef ─╫─	A symbol used for music notation when no precise reference to pitch is needed.	22*ff*
noise	Sound resulting from nonperiodic vibration.	2
nonperiodic pulses	A series of pulses of unequal duration.	14*ff*, 37
notation	The use of written symbols to represent musical sounds.	19*ff*, 52*ff*
note	Symbol used to communicate duration and pitch.	19*ff*, 65
notehead ○ ○ ●	The part of a note used to indicate pitch and/or duration.	19
octave names	A system for naming the notes and pitches throughout the piano keyboard range.	61, 62
8*va*	A symbol indicating pitches should be performed an octave higher or lower than written.	68, 188*n*
original configuration	The basic form of a configuration.	157*ff*
ostinato	A configuration persistently repeated, usually at the same pitch and in the lower part, as an accompaniment.	151*n*
overtone scale	A scale formed from the combination of a Type 4 plus a Type 2 tetrachord joined by a half step.	138
pace	The speed of pulse. See also *tempo*.	15*ff*
palindrome	A word, phrase, or configuration that reads the same backward as forward, as "madam."	165
parallel scales	Scales that share the same tonic, as for example, C major and C minor.	127
parameters	The controllable elements of music: rhythm, harmony, melody, form, and color.	9, 10
pattern	See *unit-pattern, rhythm-pattern*.	
pentatonic scale	A five-tone scale within the octave, for example, the five black keys played consecutively.	104*n*

performance practice	Standard procedures for playing music of a certain period or style.	167
periodic pulses	A series of pulses of equal duration.	14*ff*, 37
permutation	A change in the order of a series of notes.	86, 159
Phrygian mode	A diatonic scale formed from the combination of a Type 3 plus a Type 3 tetrachord joined by a whole step, for example, white keys E to E.	105, 115
piano p	Soft.	187
pianissimo pp	Very soft.	187
pianississmo ppp	As soft as possible.	187
Picardy third	A raised third scale member in the final tonic triad of a composition in a minor mode.	123
pitch	A term used to refer to the highness or lowness of a sound.	2, 52*ff*, 182*ff*
pitch class	Pitches of the same letter name and with frequencies in such ratios as 1:2, 1:4, 1:8, etc. For example, C1, C2, C3, etc. are all members of the same pitch class.	52*n*
pitch set	An ordered collection of pitches.	151
più mosso	A direction to increase the pace; literally, "more motion."	199
poco a poco	"little by little," or gradually.	189
polyphonic	Musical texture characterized by the combination of two or more melodic lines. See also *monophonic, homophonic*.	9*n*, 102
portato 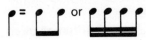	A term used to indicate that tones are to be sustained but slightly more disconnected than *legato*.	193, 194
presto	A fast tempo—faster than *allegro* but slower than *prestissimo*.	199
prestissimo	The fastest possible tempo.	199
prime	See *interval*.	
pulse	The recurring beat in music.	14*ff*
quality of chord	Characterization of a chord in terms of the specific intervals used (major triad, minor triad, major or minor seventh chord, etc.).	85*ff*
quality of interval	Characterization of an interval as major, minor, perfect, augmented, diminished, etc.	76*ff*
rallentando (rall.)	A term used to indicate a slowing of tempo.	200
real inversion	Inversion by specific interval.	157
real sequence	A sequence in which melodic intervals are repeated exactly.	159
regular division	The fractional partitioning of undotted notes into groups of twos, fours, eights and sixteens:	21, 22

Also, the partitioning of dotted notes into threes, sixes, and twelves:

See also *irregular division*.

related scales	Scales whose tones are the same but whose tonics are different, as for example, C major and D *Dorian*.	127
relative scales	Major and minor scales whose tonics are related by a minor third, as for example, C major and A minor.	127
restatement	Repetition of a configuration or segment either exactly or with varying degreees of change.	155*ff*
rests	Symbols used to denote certain amounts of silence.	19*ff*
retrograde	The technique of varying a configuration or segment by writing it backwards.	157*ff*
retrograde inversion	The technique of varying a configuration or segment by writing the melodic inversion backwards.	157*ff*
rhythm	The temporal parameter of music.	9, 13*ff*, 157*ff*
ryhthm-pattern	Two or more unit-patterns.	14
ritardando (*rit.* or *ritard.*)	A gradual decrease in tempo.	200
rondo form	A form in which restatements alternate with contrasting sections.	154
rubato	Expressive fluctuation of tempo.	200
scale	An arrangement of successive, ordered tones (low to high or high to low), usually within an octave, having a fixed pattern of intervals between tones. The number of tones and the specific pattern of intervals determine the type of scale: major, minor, pentatonic, chromatic, etc. See also *diatonic scale*.	9, 104*ff*, 113*ff*
score	A music manuscript that shows all parts of an ensemble, vertically arranged.	100
segment (s)	A part of a configuration.	157*ff*
sempre	Always, or continually—used with a term such as *staccato, legato, forte*, etc.	187*n*
sequence	The immediate repetition of a configuration or segment at a different pitch level.	159
seventh chord	A vertical sonority of four tones built in thirds.	9
sharp	A symbol that alters a natural pitch by raising it one half step. See also *alteration signs*.	57
simile (*sim.*)	In a similar manner.	194
simple intervals	Intervals of an octave or less.	81
slur	A curved line connecting notes of different pitch, indicating performance without any break between pitches.	105

sonata-allegro form	A large, first movement form generally used in the classical and romantic concerto, sonata, and symphony.	154
sound spectrum	A graph showing the distribution and intensities of the harmonics of a tone.	3, 4, 5
sound wave	Energy produced by a vibrating medium.	2
specific interval	An interval classified according to exact pitch differences.	75*ff*
spectrum	See *sound spectrum*.	
spill	See *fall-off*.	
staccatissimo ⸲	A term used to indicate that tones are to be played very short.	193, 194
staccato ⸱	A term used to indicate that notes are to be played short.	193, 194
stem	The part of a note whose duration is less than a whole note.	19
staff ≣	The five lines and resultant four spaces upon which music is written. The grand staff has two five-line staffs joined. See also *grand staff*.	65*ff*
stress	The application of emphasis to a particular musical sound.	14
stringendo (*string.*)	A gradual increase in tempo.	200
structural tones	Harmonically and/or melodically significant tones in a line. They are usually chord tones.	106
subdominant	The fourth tone of a diatonic scale.	106
subito	Suddenly or immediately; often used with an intensity level such as p or f.	189
subject	An initial configuration that is used as a basic structural element in a composition, usually a fugue. See also *fugue*.	178
submediant	The sixth tone of a diatonic scale.	106
subtonic	The seventh tone of a diatonic scale (major second below the tonic). See also *leading tone*.	107
supertonic	The second tone of a diatonic scale.	106
tempo	The pace of music; speed of pulse.	5, 15*ff*, 36*ff*, 182, 199, 200
tempo giusto	In strict tempo, the opposite of *rubato*.	199
tempo primo	A term used to indicate a return to the original tempo.	199
temporal arts	Art forms that have a time dimension (e.g., music, dance, cinema) as opposed to those with a spatial dimension alone (e.g., sculpture, painting).	154
tenuto ⸱̄	A term used to indicate that tones are to be sustained but slightly more disconnected than *portato*.	193, 194

tenor clef	A symbol designating the fourth line of the five-line staff as C4 or middle C. See also *alto clef, bass clef, neutral clef, treble clef.*	67, 70
ternary form	A three-part form.	154
tertian system	The construction of chords by the vertical stacking of thirds.	85*ff*
tetrachord	A set of four consecutive tones in a special scheme of intervals that produces part of a diatonic scale.	9, 113*ff*
texture	The vertical arrangement or the "thickness" or "thinness" of sounds. See also *homophonic, monophonic, polyphonic.*	9
tie	A curved line connecting two notes of the same pitch to indicate durational extension.	23
timbre	A characteristic of musical tone referring to the quality of the sound.	2, 3, 4, 5, 182, 200, 201
tonal center	See *key center.*	
tonal inversion	Inversion using general intervals and maintaining the tonality.	157
tonal sequence	A sequence in which the tones conform to the scale.	159
tonality	The perceived adhesiveness of a group of tones, such as those belonging to a specific key, and dominated by a tonal center. See also *key center.*	57, 106, 135*ff*
tone	Sound in the musical sense, hence a basic building block of music.	2
tone cluster	Simultaneous sounding of a group of tones in close relationship, usually in half steps.	53
tone color	See *timbre.*	
tonic	The first tone of a diatonic scale.	104, 106
tonic center	The tonal center. See also *key center.*	106
transposition	Relocation of notation to a different pitch level from the original.	105, 123, 127*ff*
treble clef	A symbol designating a note on the second line of the five-line staff as G4. See also *alto clef, bass clef, neutral clef, tenor clef.*	67*ff*, 69, 70
triad	A vertical sonority of three tones usually built in thirds.	9, 85*ff*, 104*n*
tritone	An interval of three consecutive whole steps (augmented fourth or diminished fifth).	77*n*
unison	See *interval.*	
unit	See *unit of beat.*	
unit of beat	The note used to represent one pulse.	14*ff*, 36*ff*
unit-pattern	A pulse sound or a group of sounds equivalent to one unit.	14, 16, 22, 29*ff*

unity	The presence of exact or slightly varied similarity in configuration that gives a composition formal design. See also *form*.	154*ff*
variant	A changed version of a configuration or segment.	157*ff*
variety	The use of contrasting material in a composition to avoid boredom that would result from too much restatement.	154*ff*
vibrato	Deliberate, regular pitch and/or intensity alteration applied by performers to alter or color a tone.	182-184
wave pattern	See *sound wave*.	10
whole steps	Intervals of two consecutive half steps. Whole steps occur between C and D, D and E, F and G, E and F♯, A♭ and B♭, etc.	53
whole-tone scale	A six-tone scale with whole steps between all adjacent members.	104*n*, 115

Appendix 2: Triad Nomenclature

TRIAD TYPE		CHORD NAME		TRADITIONAL* ABBREVIATION	MUSIC EXAMPLE
NAME	ABBREVIATED	NAME	ABBREVIATED		
Major	M	C major	C	C	
Minor	m	C minor	c (Cm)	Cm	
Diminished	d	C diminished	c° (Cdim)	Cdim†	
Augmented	A+	C augmented	C+	C+	

---

*　　These are the symbols most often used in popular music or jazz.

†　　The symbol (Cdim) is also used to indicate the diminished seventh chord.

Appendix 3: Source Material for Developing Music Literacy

SIGHT SINGING

Edgar Crowe, Annie Lawton, and W. Gillies Whittaker, *The Folk Song Series*, Books I-XII. New York: Oxford University Press, 1933.

Arnold Fish and Norman Lloyd, *Fundamentals of Sight Singing and Ear Training*. New York: Dodd Mead & Company, 1964.

Paul Harder, *Fundamentals of Music Reading*. New York: Belwin-Mills Publishing Corp., 1954.

Allen Irvine McHose and Ruth Northrup Tibbs, *Sight-Singing Manual*. New York: Appleton-Century-Crofts, Inc., 1957.

Robert W. Ottman, *Music For Sight Singing*. Englewood Cliffs, N.J.: Prentice-Hall, Inc., 1956.

William Thomson, *Introduction to Music Reading*. Belmont, California: Wadsworth Publishing Co., Inc., 1966.

Charles W. Walton and Harry Robert Wilson, *Music Reading Through Singing*. Belmont, California: Wadsworth Publishing Co., Inc., 1966.

EAR TRAINING

Guy Alan Brockmon and William J. Starr, *Perceiving Music: Problems in Sight and Sound* (with tape recording). New York: Harcourt Brace & World, Inc., 1962.

James C. Carlsen, *Melodic Perception* (self-instruction with tape recording). New York: McGraw-Hill Company, 1965.

Janet McLoud McGaughey, *Practical Ear Training* (manual and workbook). Boston: Allyn and Bacon, Inc., 1961.

Janet McLoud McGaughey, *Sounds of Music: Descending Intervals*. Boston: Allyn and Bacon, Inc., 1961.

Janet McLoud McGaughey, *Sounds of Music: Ascending Intervals*. Boston: Allyn and Bacon, Inc., 1961.

Robert W. Sherman and Morris H. Knight, *Aural Comprehension in Music* (two volumes with workbooks and tape recordings). New York: McGraw-Hill Book Co., 1972.

Charles L. Spohn and B. William Poland, *Sounds of Music: Harmonic Intervals*. Englewood Cliffs, N.J.: Prentice-Hall, Inc., 1967.

JAZZ IMPROVISATION

David Baker, *Jazz Improvisation: A Comprehensive Method of Study For All Players*. Chicago: Maher Publications, 1969. Distributed by db/Music Workshop Publications, Down Beat, 222 West Adams Street, Chicago, Ill. 60606.

Jerry Coker, *Improvising Jazz*. Englewood Cliffs, N.J.: Prentice-Hall, Inc., 1964.

John Mehegan, *Jazz Improvisation* (Vols. I-IV). New York: Watson-Guptill Publications, 1959-65. Distributed by Music Sales Corp., 33 W 60th St., New York, N.Y. 10023.

Appendix 4:
Answers to CYU's

The student is urged to answer all questions completely before consulting these answer keys. In cases where two or more answers are possible, the preferred answer is given first and alternatives are included in parentheses.

INTRODUCTION, NO. 1, PAGE 7

1. strings, bars, membranes, reeds, columns of air, oscillators
2. periodic (regular)
3. pitch, intensity, timbre, duration
4. high
5. hertz, Hz
6. intensity
7. vibrations
8. greater
9. decibels, db
10. timbre, tone color
11. fundamental, harmonic series
12. duration
13. decibel, amplitude, loudness

INTRODUCTION, NO. 2, PAGE 11

1. rhythm, harmony, melody, form, color
2. variation in pitch, variation in tempo, variation in duration, variation in intensity, variation in tone color
3. harmony
4. melody
5. form
6. color
7. tempo, meter, pulse

CHAPTER 1, NO. 1, PAGE 17

1. the combined effect of all factors contributing to the organized flow of sound and silence durations in time
2. the basic temporal element in a music event (beat)
3. unequal (nonperiodic)
4. tempo
5. tempo (pace)
6. a pulse-sound or a group of sounds equivalent to one pulse
7. a group of sounds made up of two or more unit-patterns
8. a) 12   b) 1, 2   c) 3, 4   4, 3   2, 6   6, 2   (any order acceptable)
9. an accurate means of selecting tempo
10. a) about 70 times per minute (could vary)
    b) about 16-20 times per minute (could vary)

    c) 64-112 steps per minute

    d) 288-336 times per minute, depending on manufacturer

11.   pulse, unit of beat, unit-pattern, rhythm-pattern, tempo, nonperiodic beat, periodic beat, metronome, accent, stress, pace

CHAPTER 1, NO. 2, PAGE 25

1.   notes

2.   rests

3.   a) notehead   b) flags   c) stem   d) noteheads   e) stems
f) beam

4.   a) sixteenth note   b) eighth rest   c) quarter rest   d) eighth note
e) half note

5.   a) quarter ♩   b) sixteenth ♬   c) half ♩   d) quarter ♩   e) eighth ♪

6.   a) 4   b) 3   c) 5   d) 1   e) 2

7.   a) eighth ♪   b) sixteenth ♬   c) eighth ♪   d) half ▬

8.   a) 2   b) 1   c) 2   d) ¼   e) 2

9.   (Compare with established norm in any printed music, or see Example 1.9.)

10.   (Compare your symbols with the models.)

11.   a) 3   b) 3   c) ¾   d) 1½   e) 3   f) 3

12. a) b) c) d) e)   13. a) b) c) d) e)

14. a) b) c)

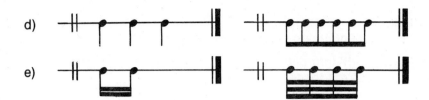

15.   note, rest, grace note, division, dotted note, pulse, regular division, tempo, unit, unit-pattern, tie, rhythm-pattern, stem, beam, dot, note value, double dot, flag, duration

CHAPTER 1, NO. 3, PAGE 33

1.   5

2.   between sections and at the end of a composition

3.   a) each measure will contain the equivalent of two eighth notes
     b) each measure will contain the equivalent of three quarter notes
     c) each measure will contain the equivalent of nine eighth notes
     d) each measure will contain the equivalent of six quarter notes
     e) each measure will contain the equivalent of seven eighth notes

4.   a) $\frac{3}{4}$ b) $\frac{3}{8}$ c) $\frac{4}{4}$ or $\frac{2}{2}$ or ¢   d) $\frac{2}{8}$

5.   a)

     b)

     c)

     d)

     e)

6.   a)   or   b)   or   c)   or   d)   or   e)   or

     f)   or   g)   or   h)   or   i)   or   j)   or

7.   measure, pulse, barline, measure signature, $\frac{2}{4}$, note

CHAPTER 1, NO. 4, PAGE 39

1. the manner in which notation is grouped, the indication of unit and tempo by the composer, the measure signature

2. the type of note that will represent one beat (pulse)

3. any musical note, dotted or undotted

4. a) 1   b) 2   c) 4   d) ¼   e) ½   f) 1/8   g) 1½   h) 3   i) ½

5. a) ♩   b) ♩·   c) ♪   d) ♩   e) ♪·

6. a) $\frac{4}{4}$ or $\frac{2}{2}$ or ¢   b) $\frac{3}{4}$ c) $\frac{3}{8}$ d) $\frac{3}{4}$ e) $\frac{2}{2}$ or ¢

7. motion, unit, conducting pattern, beam, measure, tempo, unit of beat

CHAPTER 2, NO. 1, PAGE 55

1. 1:2 (2:1)   2. 524, 131

3. 12   4. A, B, C, D, E, F, G

5. 2, 3

6.

7. 1/12   8. 1/6

9. E and F, B and C

10. A and B, C and D, D and E, F and G, G and A

11. 7

12. C and D, D and E, F and G, G and A, A and B

13. chromatic

14. equal temperament, frequency, octave, Hz, scale, interval, half step, diatonic, middle C, A = 440, tone cluster, chromatic scale

CHAPTER 2, NO. 2, PAGE 59

1. a) natural   b) sharp   c) flat   d) double sharp   e) double flat

2. alteration signs

3.   a) sharp ♯   b) flat ♭   c) natural ♮   d) natural ♮

4.   D♭♭, D♭, D♮, D♯, D𝄪   5.   half step

6.   two (2), four (4)   7.   before

8.   (Compare your symbols with the models.)

9.

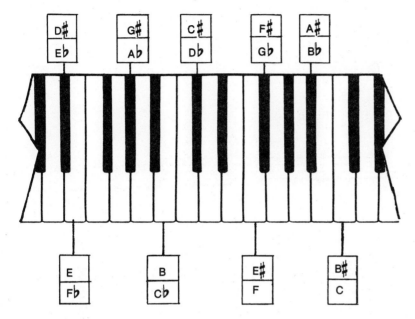

10.   enharmonic

11.   a) E♭   b) D♯   c) F♯   d) B♭   e) G♯   f) A♭   g) C♮   h) B♯

        i) E♮   j) A♯   k) B♮   l) C♯   m) D♮   n) E♭♭   o) D♮   p) G♮

        q) F♮   r) A♮

12.   sharp, natural, double flat, enharmonic spelling, double sharp

CHAPTER 2, NO. 3, PAGE 63

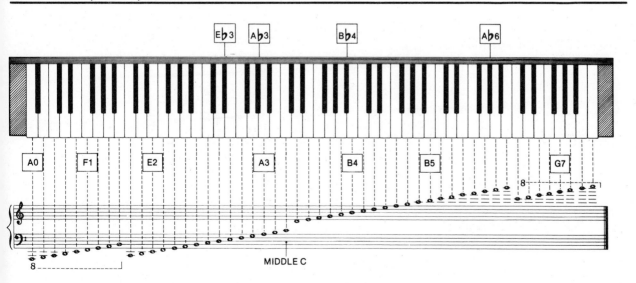

CHAPTER 2, NO. 4, PAGE 71

1.   (Compare your symbols with the models.)

2.   a) treble, G   b) alto, C   c) bass, F

3.   (Compare your symbols with the models.)

4.   C, D, E, C, B, F, A, C, A, B, F, G, C, F, D

5.   C, B, D, E, G, A, B, G, A, B, E

6.   C, F, E, B, F, G, E, D, E, A, C; tenor

7.   F, E, G, A, B, G, E, C, C, F, D

8.   C4, C4, G3, G4, D5, D3, A2, A5, F5, F3, B3

9.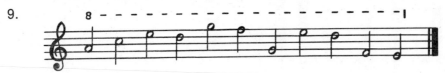

10.

11.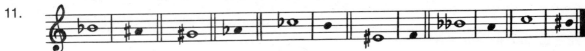

12.   A4, C1, G♯6, staff, grand staff, C clef, staff lines, clef signs, ascending pitches, ledger lines, tenor clef, bass clef, *8va*, *15ma*

CHAPTER 2, NO. 5, PAGE 79

1.

2.

3.

4. a) perfect: primes, fourths, fifths, octaves
   b) major: seconds, thirds, sixths, sevenths
   c) minor: seconds, thirds, sixths, sevenths
   d) augmented: fourths, fifths, octaves, primes, seconds, thirds, sixths, sevenths
   e) diminished: fourths, fifths, octaves, seconds, thirds, sixths, sevenths

5. minor   6. diminished

7. augmented   8. diminished

9. raising the lower note a half step

10. a) 1   b) 3½   c) ½   d) 2½   e) 3   f) 1½

11. P5, M2, A5, A8, A4, M6, M7, M3, m3, M9, A6, P1

12.

13.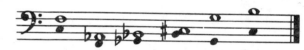

14. general interval, perfect octave, specific interval, primes, diminished fifth, major sixth, tritone, perfect fifth, interval quality

CHAPTER 2, NO. 6, PAGE 83

1. a) octave   b) seventh   c) sixth   d) fifth   e) fourth   f) third
   g) second   h) prime

2. a)

   b)

3.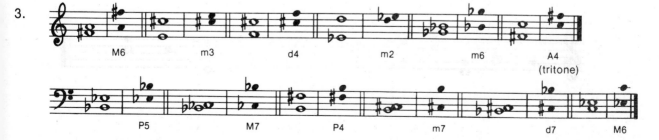

4.   M6, P5, inversion, specific interval, simple, A4, compound, harmonic interval, seventh, tenth, tritone

CHAPTER 2, NO. 7, PAGE 91

1.   major triads, minor triads

2.   A triad is a vertical sonority of three tones. These tones are arranged in thirds in the tertian system of harmony.

3.   a) major third (M3)   b) minor third (m3)   c) perfect fifth (P5)

4.   a) minor third (m3)   b) major third (M3)   c) perfect fifth (P5)

5.   a) minor third (m3)   b) minor third (m3)   c) diminished fifth (d5)

6.   a) major third (M3)   b) major third (M3)   c) augmented fifth (A5)

7.   third   8.   root

9.   See Example 2.34.

10. A C♯ E   D F♯ A   G B D   E♭ G B♭   D♭ F A♭

     D♯ F𝄪 A♯   G♭ B♭ D♭   B♭ D F   B D♯ F♯   C E G

11. A C E   B D F♯   B♭ D♭ F   E♭ G♭ B♭   C E♭ G

     D♭ F♭ A♭   E♭ G♭ B♭   D F A   B D F♯   D♯ F♯ A♯

12. C E♭ G♭   D F A♭   C♯ E G   E♭ G♭ B♭♭   E G B♭

     E♯ G♯ B   E G B♭   F♯ A C   G♯ B D   A C E♭

13. C E G♯   D♭ F A   D F♯ A♯   D F♯ A♯   E♭ G B

     F A C♯   G♭ B♭ D   G B D♯   A♭ C E   A C♯ E♯

14. A M M m m d d M M A M A

     F+   G B♭ f f♯ g♯° c° A♭ D A♭+ G♭ B♭+

     M A m m d m M M M M d M

     A A+ d b♭ g° c E♭ B G C♭ g♯°   B♭

15.

16. seventh chord, triad, basic triad, root, chord third, chord fifth, diminished triad, major triad, e°, minor chord, augmented triad, G +, chord quality

CHAPTER 3, NO. 1, PAGE 109

1.   Melody is an orderly, horizontal succession of tones perceived as the dominating line.

2. eight, half, whole; tonic, eighth; A, B, C, D, E, F, G, five, two; half steps

3. tonic   4.   seven (7)

5. a) Aeolian   b) Locrian   c) Ionian   d) Dorian   e) Phrygian
    f) Lydian   g) Mixolydian

6. a) C   b) C   c) B   d) F   e) G   f) C

7.

Ionian

8. (your choice)

9. a) tonic   b) supertonic   c) mediant   d) subdominant   e) dominant
    f) submediant   g) leading tone, subtonic   h) tonic

10. a) A6, P5, P5, M3, M2, m3, P4, A4
    b) d5, m7, M7, P8, P5, P5, A4, A6
    c) P1, A1, m2, M2, M9, A2, m3, M3
    d) m7, A2, d3, P5, M9, M3, d5, P8

11. diatonic, chromatic, tonic, M6, P4, Aeolian, whole tone scale, Ionian mode,
    Phrygian, octave, mode, dominant, subtonic, leading tone, derived scale

CHAPTER 3, NO. 2, PAGE 117

1. a) C, D, E, F   b) D, E, F, G   c) E, F, G, A   d) F, G, A, B
    e) G, A, B, C   f) A, B, C, D   g) B, C, D, E

2. lower   3.   upper

4. four (4)

5.

6. Type 1 ● ● ● ●   Type 3 ● ● ● ●

    Type 2 ● ● ● ●   Type 4 ● ● ● ●

7.   diatonic, whole, half step

8.   Two Type 4 tetrachords joined by a whole step would exceed an octave and thus violate the definition of a diatonic scale.

9.   a) C, D, E, F, G, A, B, C; Ionian   b) D, E, F, G, A, B, C, D; Dorian
     c) A, B, C, D, E, F, G, A; Aeolian   d) E, F, G, A, B, C, D, E; Phrygian
     e) G, A, B, C, D, E, F, G; Mixolydian

10. Locrian   11.   Lydian

12. whole tone (extended beyond the octave)

13. 1, 1; C, D, E, F, G, A, B, C

14. a) G♯, A, B, C♯, D♯, E, F♯, G♯; Phrygian

     b) B♭, C, D, E♭, F, G, A, B♭; Ionian

     c) B♭, C, D, E♭, F, G, A♭, B♭; Mixolydian

     d) F♯, G♯, A, B, C♯, D♯, E, F♯; Dorian

     e) B♭, C, D♭, E♭, F, G, A♭, B♭; Dorian

     f) A♭, B♭, C, D♭, E♭, F, G, A♭; Ionian

     g) E, F♯, G, A, B, C, D, E; Aeolian

     h) F, G, A♭, B♭, C, D♭, E♭, F; Aeolian

     i) A, B♭, C, D, E, F, G, A; Phrygian

15. a) Mixolydian

     b) Ionian

     c) Dorian

     d) Aeolian

     e) Lydian

     f) Phrygian

16. half step, tetrachord, whole step, Type 1 tetrachord, interval, Dorian tetrachord, Phrygian tetrachord, Lydian tetrachord, diatonic scale, Mixolydian mode, Dorian mode, Lydian mode

CHAPTER 3, NO. 3, PAGE PAGE 125

1.   major, harmonic minor   2.   leading tone

3.   a) A, B, C, D, E, F, G, A; Aeolian   b) B, C, D, E, F, G, A, B; Locrian
     c) C, D, E, F, G, A, B, C; Ionian   d) D, E, F, G, A, B, C, D; Dorian

e) E, F, G, A, B, C, D, E; Phrygian   f) F, G, A, B, C, D, E, F; Lydian
g) G, A, B, C, D, E, F, G; Mixolydian

4. Ionian; 1, 1

5. major

6.
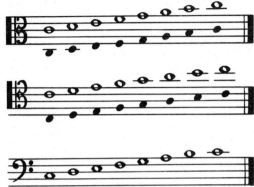

7. 2

8. fourth (4th), lowered

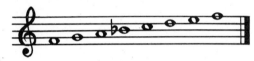

9. minor

10. raised seventh (7th)

    harmonic

11. sixth, lowering the seventh

12.

13. major

14. minor

15. octave, upper tetrachord, Type 1, diatonic tetrachord, lower tetrachord, C-major scale, Aeolian minor, major modes

CHAPTER 3, NO. 4, PAGE 131

1. 12; F, G♭ (or F♯), G, A♭ (or G♯), A, B♭ (or A♯), B, C, D♭ (or C♯)

2. one; one; F♯; C♯; perfect fifth

3. two, F♯, C♯; three, F♯, C♯, G♯

4. flat (♭); one; B♭; E♭; perfect fifth

5. one, B♭; two, B♭, E♭; three, B♭, E♭, A♭; BEAD

6.

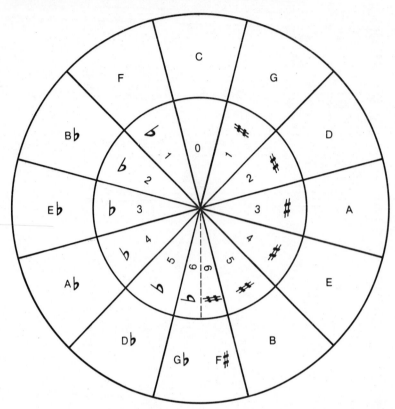

(Any circular arrangement including the above information would be acceptable.)

7. F♯, C♯, G♯, D♯, A♯, E♯, B♯   8.   B♭, E♭, A♭, D♭, G♭, C♭, F♭

9. C♯, C♭

10. one; one; F♯; one, B♭; one; B♭, E♭

11. A minor, D minor, E minor, G major, E♭ major

12. A minor, D major

13. a) F♯   b) F♯, C♯   c) F♯, C♯, G♯   d) B♭   e) B♭, E♭   f) F♯

    g) F♯, C♯   h) B♭   i) B♭, E♭   j) B♭, E♭, A♭, D♭   k) F♯   l) B♭

    m) F♯, C♯, G♯, D♯

14. a) Aeolian on E

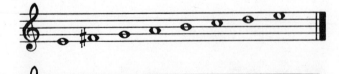

    b) Mixolydian on C

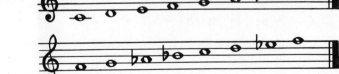

    c) Dorian on F

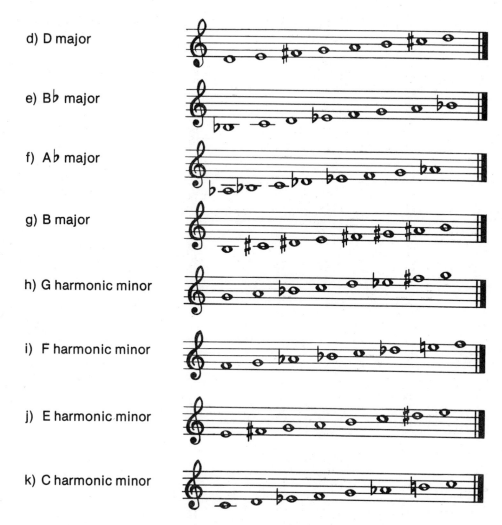

d) D major

e) B♭ major

f) A♭ major

g) B major

h) G harmonic minor

i) F harmonic minor

j) E harmonic minor

k) C harmonic minor

15.   circle of fifths, relative minor, parallel minor, relative major, Aeolian form, Mixolydian on D, E-major scale, Dorian on G, G Dorian

CHAPTER 3, NO. 5, PAGE 139

1.   identify the basic set of sharps or flats used in a specific tonality

2.   all octave equivalents

3.   that specific pitch for the duration of the measure

4.   F♯, C♯, G♯, D♯, A♯, E♯, B♯   5.   B♭, E♭, A♭, D♭, G♭, C♭, F♭

6.   yes   7.   no

8.   a) G major   b) G minor

c) A major

d) E♭ major

e) E major

f) A♭ major

g) B major

h) D♭ major

i) C♯ major

j) C♭ major

k) E minor

l) C minor

m) C♯ minor

n) D minor

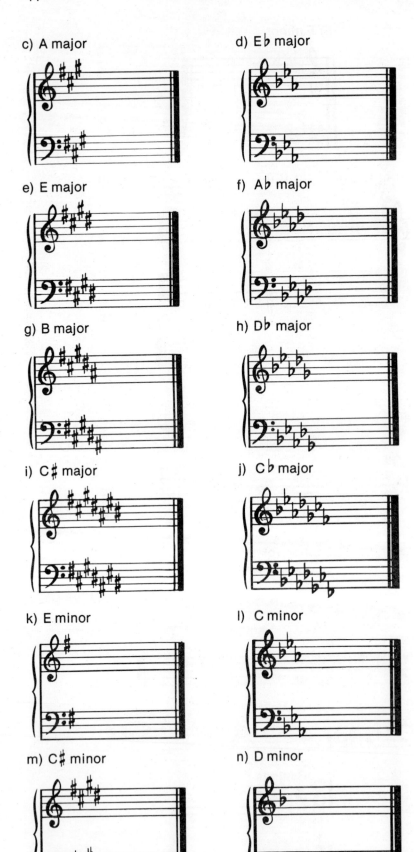

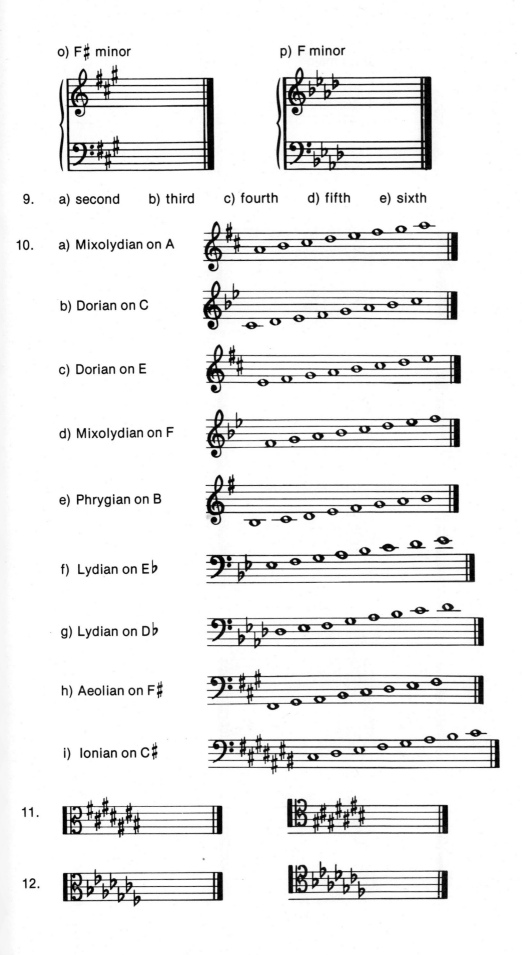

o) F♯ minor

p) F minor

9.   a) second   b) third   c) fourth   d) fifth   e) sixth

10.   a) Mixolydian on A

b) Dorian on C

c) Dorian on E

d) Mixolydian on F

e) Phrygian on B

f) Lydian on E♭

g) Lydian on D♭

h) Aeolian on F♯

i) Ionian on C♯

11.

12.

13.   key signatures, key center, tonic center, tonality, key of F, five-flat signature, modulate, predominating tonality

CHAPTER 4, NO. 1, PAGE 163

1.   Form is the organizational structure of music and results from the logical growth of the initial musical gesture, idea, or configuration.

2.   a) contrast   b) variety

3.   configuration, unity, variety, restatement, contrast, balance, repetition, development, variant, retrograde, inversion, retrograde inversion, sequence, segment, augmentation, diminution, expansion, contraction, fugue, canon, ostinato, palindrome, musical gesture, deletion, interpolation, melodic expansion, texture, transposition

4.   retrograde, inversion, retrograde inversion

5.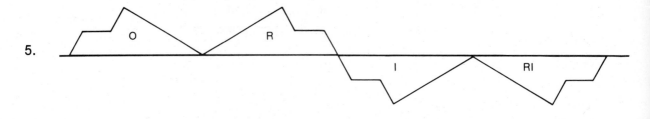

6.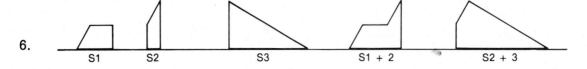

7.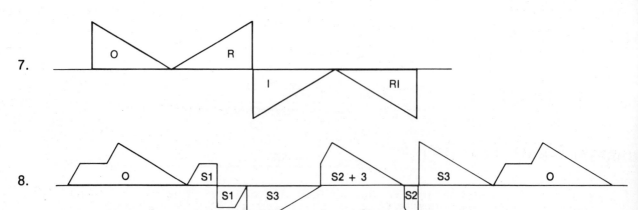

8.

9.   12

10.

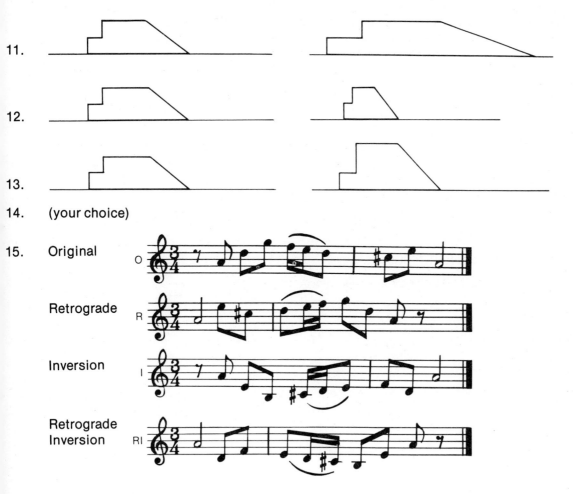

11.

12.

13.

14.   (your choice)

15.   Original

Retrograde

Inversion

Retrograde
Inversion

CHAPTER 4, NO. 2, PAGE 169

1.   your choice, but could include: composer's intent, analysis, knowledge of
      music structure, musical gestures, melodic material, restatement, contrast,
      interpretation, phrasing, accompanying material, unity, variety, symmetry,
      balance, style, details of structure

2.   Ostinatos should generally be subordinate to melodic configurations.

CHAPTER 4, NO. 3, PAGE 173

1.   your choice, but could include: configuration identification, repetition,
      contrast, memory, rest point, perceived musical events, expectation, the whole
      composition, aural imagery, aural acuity, repeated listening, analysis,
      development of configuration

2.   repetitive, boring

3.   full of contrast, difficult to unify, too varied

4.   Preference probably should be for a balance between the two extremes of unity
      and contrast.

5.   unity, variety, restatement, balance, binary, musical gesture, design, configuration, repetition, retrograde inversion, original, inversion, segment, retrograde, tonal inversion, real inversion, augmentation, sequence, diminution, contraction, ostinato, vertical expansion, interpolation, deletion, palindrome

CHAPTER 5, NO. 1, PAGE 185

1.   Color is variety of expression.

2.   pitch, tempo, duration, intensity, timbre

3.   The equal temperament tuning system produces twelve (12) half steps to the octave.

4.   Vibrato is a deliberate pitch fluctuation above and below the desired pitch

5.   timbre, vibrato, bend, fall-off, harmonics, nonvibrato, pitch fluctuation

CHAPTER 5, NO. 2, PAGE 191

1.   Intensity is the level of loudness.

2.   steady level of intensity, changing level of intensity

3.   a) *pp*   b) ———≡ *cresc. crescendo*   c) ≡——— *dim. diminuendo*
      d) *f*   e) *mp*   *mf*

4.
      Soft   Loud
      ppp   *pp*   *p*   *mp*   *mf*   *f*   *ff*   *fff*

5.

6.   decibel, dynamic level, *mezzo piano, forte, crescendo, dim.*, *mf, pp,* ———— , *subito p, poco a poco cresc.*

CHAPTER 5, NO. 3, PAGE 197

1. Different effects are obtained by altering note lengths for expressive purposes.

2. note length, note connection

3. a) *legato* - smooth and connected
    b) *portato* - slightly shorter than legato and disconnected
    c) *staccato* - short, but not the shortest
    d) *fermata* - hold for extra duration
    e) *tenuto* - long, but disconnected

4.

5. *staccato, tenuto, portato,*  , slur, , articulation

CHAPTER 5, NO. 4, PAGE 203

1. a) *rubato* - allowing the tempo to fluctuate purposely for expressive effect
    b) *presto* - very fast
    c) *adagio* - slower than *andante* but faster than *lento*
    d) *andante* - a moderate, walking tempo
    e) *lento* - quite slow but not as slow as *largo*

2. *Rubato* is used for only temporary fluctuation in tempo but should not distend the overall musical time. A slowing down should be offset by a speeding up. *Rubato* should be used sparingly.

3. English and foreign terms for tempo speed are vague and subject to vast differences in meaning when it comes to beats per minute. The tempo-unit method, using metronome indications, is safest to insure that the performance follows the musical intent.

4. a) *largo*   b) *lento*   c) *adagio*   d) *andante*   e) *allegro*   f) *presto*

5.

6.

7.

8.   *meno mosso, tempo primo, rubato, accel., rit., stringendo, rall.,* muted